THE WORKER, ALONE!
PRAISE FOR DR. FISHER'S...

WORK WITHOUT MANAGERS
A VIEW FROM THE TRENCHES

"Fisher opens angrily by declaring that 'any large company today is 20 to 30 divisions in search of a corporation.' He asserts that six 'silent killers' afflict corporate progress. A Dallas Morning News columnist called it 'the most insightful, perceptive examination of the American workplace today.'"

—**Dr. Thomas L. Brown**, editor, Industry Week

"By reading this book managers can discover why professionals are discontent with the way they are being treated and how they show their contempt. This book can be recommended for managers whether situated in the U.S., or elsewhere, because of the invaluable insights provided with regard to the professional employee and the problems with organizations."

—**Gerlinde Konrad**, Bucher Perspektiven (Austria)

"White-collar crime? Fisher argues that organizational management has not been and will not be the driving influence behind the dramatic turnaround that is needed to get this country back on track. The problem rides on the American organization's inability to manage, motivate and mobilize the professional/technical worker to productive effort."

—Training & Development Journal

"Work Without Managers is a major work of 1991. It is our opinion that Fisher has more than accomplished his goal (to stimulate discussion and debate), and that Work promises to foster a controversy that will be instrumental in affecting a fundamental change in the American workplace."

—**Jagdish N. Sheth**, Business Book Review Journal

PURPOSEFUL SELLING (FORMERLY CONFIDENT SELLING FOR THE 90'S)

"Confident Selling for the 90's* contains a wealth of information, some about the past and present, but much more on future directions. It could turn out to be as prophetic as John Naisbitt's Megatrends. It says that in the future, jobs will be focused on the talents and efforts of teams or 'cells,' rather than having an individual getting all the credit (and the money) which is really the result of support staff, too."

—New Awareness Magazine

"Dr. Fisher feels that the psychology of selling is undergoing a transformation and offers a remarkable guide to better opportunities, a better self-image and better sales. Not just for sales people, the book is a veritable road map to ever-increasing success."

—Arizona Networking News

*Confident Selling for the 90s was a Pulitzer Prize nominee for nonfiction in 1992.

The Worker, Alone!
Going Against the Grain

"There is only one word to describe The Worker, Alone! — Awesome!"

—**William L. Livingston**, author, The New Plague and Friends in High Places

"This book needs to be read. It is not however a subject to 'win friends and influence people,' but does provide the seeds of the needed changes which have to be planted if we are ever to go forward."

—**Stanley Reeves**, Educator

"I have just surmised what constitutes an important book: one written by Dr. Fisher, which proves embarrassing because it makes us think about things we would otherwise prefer to ignore."

—**Gary Herrity**, Principal, Horace Mann Elementary, Clinton, Iowa

THE ASCENT OF THE WORKING WOMAN

James R. Fisher, Jr., Ph.D.

ALSO BY JAMES R. FISHER, JR.

- *Confident Selling*
- *Work Without Managers*
- *Confident Selling for the 90s*
- *Purposeful Selling*
- *The Taboo Against Being Your Own Best Friend*
- *Meet Your New Best Friend*
- *Six Silent Killers*
- *Corporate Sin*
- *In the Shadow of the Courthouse (novel)*
- *A Look Back to See Ahead*
- *Time Out for Sanity!*
- *Confident Thinking*
- *A Green Island in a Black Sea (novel)*
- *Who Put You in the Cage?*
- *Self-Confidence: The Elusive Key to Health, Happiness & Emotional Survival*
- *A Way of Thinking About Things!*
- *Nowhere Man in Nowhere Land*
- *The Worker, Alone! Going Against the Grain*

Always to Beautiful Betty

&

George Edward Daly of Calgary, Alberta Canada

"For the past quarter century we have had a bombardment of ideas on how to manage change. Actually, change in the workplace is of only secondary importance. Change will come about naturally, over time, once workers and managers bring about change in themselves. Order comes from within. To establish order takes more than good intentions, more than a change of attitude. Order requires a radical change in mentality, a structural change in how workers and managers view the world. Such radicalism requires the individual going against the grain."

James R. Fisher, Jr., **The Worker, Alone! Going Against The Grain** (1995)

At times, the historian would have been almost willing to maintain that the man had overthrown the Church chiefly because it was feminine. After the overthrow of the Church, the woman had no refuge except such as the man created for himself. She was free; she had no illusions; she was sexless; she had discarded all that the male disliked; and although she secretly regretted the discard, she knew that she could not go backward. She must, like the man, marry machinery.

Henry Adams, **The Education of Henry Adams** (1905)

CONTENTS

THE INTRODUCTION

    About "The Ascent of the Working Woman!"

    Introduction: 21" Century Reality Check

    The New Old Plague

    Going Against the Grain

    The Need for Clear Thinking

THE FEMININE PARADIGM

    An Upside Down World!
    Silent Invasions!
    The Price Of Innocence!
    Late Blooming Roses!
    The Life without Cause!
    Ascendency of the Paradigm

THE MASCULINE PARADIGM

> Architects of a Failed System!
> Not Happy Campers! .
> The Challenge of Learning!
> A Question of Control!
> Why Embracing a Paradigm Shift Is So Rare

EMPIRICAL EVIDENCE OF THE SHIFT,

> A Career-Changing Personal Brief
> Going Against the Grain!
> A Leadership Manifesto

CONCLUSION

> Conversation with Stanley Reeves!

SELECTIVE BIBLIOGRAPHY

ABOUT THE AUTHOR

JAMES R. FISHER, JR., Ph.D.
© December 25, 2017

INTRODUCTION

ABOUT "THE ASCENT OF THE WORKING WOMAN"

German philosopher and jurist Hermann Kantorowicz (1877 – 1940) considers ideas as weapons. He writes, *"There is an important distinction between thoughts and ideas. Men possess thoughts. Ideas possess men."* French novelist Victor Hugo (1802 – 1885) is even more provocative insisting, *"Men have sight, women have insight."*

"The Ascent of the Working Woman" is a journey of ideas that tracks such sentiments. If you sense that something is amiss, but can't put your finger on it, Dr. Fisher will guide you through the trivia that passes for knowledge to show mythical gender and cultural clashes that consume so much of our attention, no longer have purchase for the working woman as we all move out of the shadow of the dying *Sensate Culture* of our magnificent past into a new *Ideational Culture* of a creative tomorrow.

Over the past seventy years, or since WWII, while familiar impediments to the working woman have been disappearing, new ideas relating to women have taken root. These ideas form the basis of *"The Ascent of the Working Woman!"*

Principally, women have risen to the fore, manifesting new prominence in what Dr. Fisher calls, *"The Feminine Paradigm"* with its accent on "right brain" thinking, complementing the *Masculine Paradigm* of "left brain" thinking—subsuming the collective *mindset* to all spheres of brain in human problem solving.

Regarding the eminent cultural shift, according to the theories of sociologist Pitirim Sorokin (1889 – 1968), we are at the end of a 600 year dying *Sensate Culture* into a transitional and transformational period toward a glorious 600 year *Ideational Culture* of the creative tomorrow.

Author Fisher urges us to recognize and embrace this new day that is now upon us. He challenges us to discard our cherished assumptions about present day work and life, and to embrace a new solidarity as men and women immersed in a common and equal partnership moving out of the shadows of obsessional materialism and self-conscious sexism into the dawn of a creative and spiritual tomorrow where instrumental and terminal values blend into common pursuits to economic, social and emotional well-being.

21ST CENTURY REALITY CHECK

THE NEW OLD PLAGUE

WHILE LITERALLY everything has changed, conditions for the working professional, that vaunted knowledge worker, have not. In shameful fashion, workplace professionals are assigned, evaluated, categorized and promoted by means of criteria intended for a time long past with protocols that have little to do with their professional potential, ethics or, incredibly, actual job requirements.

Inexplicably, "modern" workplace professionals are managed, motivated, mobilized and manipulated in conformance with a long outdated model, a model characterized by *position power,* hierarchies, ritualistic routines and restrictive practices that contribute little to the bottom line; to the contrary actually.

In part, we can blame this on the unrelenting explosion in technology, which has accelerated since *The Worker, Alone!* was first published in 1995. This tsunami of technology resulted in spiraling costs to employers and constant coping by workers. Call it an enormous distraction. If the obvious purpose of a company is "what it does," and "what it does" is simply cosmetic housekeeping, not aligned change with corporate objectives, then it becomes a serious problem, and it has.

Meanwhile, against this backdrop of coping with new technology, the corporate "system" engages tenaciously in *business as usual* practices with implacable authority, despite setback after setback. It operates as a *knowing* rather than a *learning* institution, disregarding valuable lessons.

Rx: For a Healthier Workplace

How then do we reawaken and revitalize a profoundly unconscious workplace? It's easy to point fingers at management, but that does not adequately address the issue. Nor does it deal with the larger problem of a devotion to the *status quo*. Workers are content to wait for someone to take charge and lift them out of their malaise while managers reprove workers for their reluctance to exercise initiative. Ironically, professional workers wait and hope for someone to lead, when it is they, alone, who possess the necessary tools and acumen. They wait, timidly, for the vested powers to finally come to their senses, when those interests have far too much invested in the current reality to gamble on change.

Meaningful change will come about only when workers, aided by managers, summon the courage to bring about change from within. There is neither an upside to hope nor a downside to courage. But make no mistake; courage is both the engine of survival and the means to prevail.

Change as a natural occurrence has its own impetus, but lacks conscious direction. It is aimless and unreliable. Change is a random variable in the work environment and thus of secondary concern. Change of the deliberate sort, needed change within the individual, comes from having a center, a central governor, and manifests as a behavioral construct.

There are pitfalls to avoid, however. Needed change takes more than a change in attitude, more than good intentions, more than catchy slogans, more than a positive work climate, or a generous confection of incentives. Necessary change requires a radical change of mindset accompanied by a structural change in the way workers and managers execute their roles and conduct their relationship vis-à-vis each other. Stated simply, it takes hard work. Favorable impressions may result, but they are not the goal.

Essential change now calls for professional workers to go against the grain, to oppose the status quo. It is time for professional workers to take charge!

How We Got Here

The corporate luxury of passively believing that "doing everything one can for workers, and in return expecting workers to be motivated to do everything they can for the company," is an extravagance companies can no longer afford. It's a strategy that has proven counterproductive to the extreme.

Entitlements and perks were expected to increase worker creativity and productivity. Instead, these confections have resulted in counter dependence and learned helplessness. When the connection between contribution and compensation was lost, workers became isolated from the reality of company dynamics, from the imperatives of daily operations in meeting the relentless demands of the marketplace.

Instead of this essential linkage, workers became reliant on the comforts delivered by management. It led to professional complacency and counter dependence on the company for workers' total well-being. These workers brought their bodies to work and left their minds at home. Captive to this chronic disorder, many companies now struggle to remain solvent and to compete in the global economy. The trend has been for companies to rely on manpower outsourcing or the use of temporary workers rather than to address the problem of corporate apathy.

Contrary to what orthodoxy insists, harmony is not the glue that holds a company on task. *Managed conflict* is. Unfortunately, employees have been conditioned to shy away from confrontation, to avoid conflict, to be safe hires, to shun risk taking of any sort, the opposite of being self-directed and engaged in collective synergy.

More than a half-century of this programming has resulted in the workforce that we have today; one largely reactive at the expense of taking the initiative. Now, when creativity is required, workers are unable or unwilling to respond. It's simply not part of their makeup. For too long, companies promoted security, and were willing to give workers everything except control of work. Lethargy, and passivity is the bitter product of this oversight.

When workers operate as renters instead of owner-stakeholders, contribution consists of safely following protocols, not productive, purposeful collaboration between workers and managers.

Dumping the Trash

Envisioning a new reality, workers and managers can be equal partners, but not until we see the following changes:

Performance Appraisal Systems (PAS) phased out. Perfunctory PAS is an elitist management practice that does nothing except reinforce *position power*. The new relationship between workers and managers is organic, fluid and interdependent. Workers pursue goals entirely consistent with overall company direction, while management provides clarity and context.

Personal reward and recognition programs for professionals (i.e., cash and prizes) eliminated. Incentives have proven to encourage bad behavior and to demotivate and divide knowledge workers, inhibiting cooperation and fostering wasteful internal competition. Workers prefer ownership of what they do provided they are given the tools to do the job, and the liberty (control) to perform the task in their own inimitable style, measured against parameters understood and agreed upon. The work is the reward for professionals.

Departmental and functional group competition suspended as overall organizational performance is emphasized. Creating discrete business units or departmental functions to compete against each other stymies creativity and leads to imitation at the expense of the overarching mission of the corporate entity.

Although counterintuitive, it is nonetheless true that when each function or department in a complex system is performing as well as it can, the overall system is not. Conversely, when these departments or functions focus on one shared objective, the organization succeeds beyond expectations. It is the nature of synergy.

Cease and desist with micromanagement. Over control creates reactionary workers. When failures occur, it is "not my problem!" They wait for management to solve the problem, when only they have the faculties and facilities to do so. Micromanagement weakens workers resolve creating a vacuum in which chaos thrives. Crisis management follows, a perpetual cycle in which management solves problems it creates, while workers take pleasure in the charade, failing to see they are also its victims. On the other hand, when workers are given ownership of what they do, they quickly resolve each issue as it arises, not waiting for management to intervene. In this work climate, chronic problems are addressed at the source.

Cease to see management as distinct from professional workers. Managers are atavistic and management, as we know it, is anachronistic, an outmoded technology. No longer are eighty (80) percent of the workforce unskilled blue-collar workers, and twenty (20) percent management and administrative support. Now, less than twenty percent of workers are unskilled while eighty percent are professionally trained. Management today is essentially everybody. Therefore, workers need to have a sense of this new role and accountability. Stated another way, this new work climate cannot be partitioned. Quality, for example, is not only a quality department function in human resources, engineering, and production, administration, sales and marketing. Quality is a matter of concern for everyone, as all functions are interdependent, part of one organic whole.

Refrain from faddism. There was a time when companies were "searching" for excellence, imitating successful companies to the nth detail. Many of these companies in the end failed. Emulation was often at the expense of a regard for their immutable uniqueness. Each company is as unique from other companies as individuals are unique from each other. Each company has a distinctive history, value and belief system, infrastructure and relational heritage, along with proprietary highs and lows, and matchless secrets.

Corporate essence stokes (internal) aspirations, manifested in its (external) propensities. As fixated as people may be, this is more the case with companies. They run on the momentum that has brought them to this time, place and space. Mergers often end poorly because this intangible cohesiveness is not considered.

The seeds for rejuvenation are never "out there!" The better wisdom for an enterprise is to create the new out of the ashes of the old. This exploits the collective mindset. The reticent majority often reveals answers concerning survival. Too frequently in panic mode, these voices are dismissed as unimportant and therefore ignored. Instead, grandiose schemes and quick fixes are entertained. They range from "hot house" training programs to cutting edge technologies to tantalizing shortcuts supposed to ensure instantaneous course corrections and cures for decade's old faux pas. Stopgap measures usually carry the seductive scent of cosmetic change, while merely postponing the inevitable. Change for change's sake is no change at all.

Finally, Professional Women as well as Men Taking Charge

Twenty years ago it was "crunch time" for workers as professionals. This was essentially ignored, as they were too busy complaining to seize the initiative. Now they inhabit a dysfunctional system that they inherited, a system they did not create, but have not improved.

A new crop of professionals is coming into the system with their heads down as well. They have invested heavily in education with a disappointing return on that investment, as good paying jobs prove difficult to find.

Once these professionals have a job, there is little sense of security as the train wrecks of conglomerates are heard in the distance. They are as angry at "the system" as were their elders, failing to realize they are the system.

This is a book predicated on the principal that nothing changes at work until men and women professionals change. Games of trendy themes like empowerment continue, because they're enticing and safe, risking nothing to those in power. It is now urgently up to workers to put this house in order. Neither house cleaning nor finger pointing will do. Professionals must get off the dime and boldly take charge of work, their work, which is the path to taking charge in life.

—**James R. Fisher, Jr., Ph.D.** © February 2, 2017

GOING AGAINST THE GRAIN

Work is changing but workers are expected to "go with the flow," maintain the status quo without misgiving. Half of all workplaces in industry and commerce have no collective bargaining. Unions are the dinosaurs of the times. While the rhetoric of empowerment rises to a crescendo, the workforce itself is more powerless in the workplace than ever before. Some actually think that a powerless workforce is the only way to have economic growth, while others feel it is the condition which will lead back to trade unionism. Neither outcome seems realistic.

THE DISEMPOWERMENT of the workforce will certainly not lead to higher economic growth, nor is it likely to lead to a rebirth of trade unionism. On the contrary; what concerns Dr. Fisher about the present climate is the unimaginativeness and inertia of management on the one hand, and the passivity with which the workforce as a whole accepts its disenfranchisement on the other.

The evidence suggests workers everywhere see themselves at the mercy of employers, bosses, "the system," and yet they do nothing. Oh, they may feign concern, but the proof is in that nothing changes. Workers deny reality, go along with things as they are, ventilate frustration on a need basis, but always at the expense of colleagues or loved ones, never at their true adversary, themselves!

The price workers' pay for disenfranchisement at work and indifference as citizens is an inflationary housing market, unsustainable consumption booms, mountains of accumulated debt and constant flirtation with economic recession. Despite miraculous maneuvering of the government, led by the Federal Reserve, this will always be the case, so long as disenfranchisement of the workforce remains representative.

Workers don't get it. They are in charge of their destiny, and don't know or want to know it. They are waiting for the "company store" to provide their staples. No matter how many times they are sideswiped by reality, no matter how often their social, economic, spiritual and emotional status rides the roller coaster, they dream of calm waters, flat playing fields and Nirvana!

Dr. Fisher punctures this dream in this brilliant essay. It is designed to show workers everywhere what is happening and why. More importantly, he brings the reader to the full realization that virtually everyone is alone; that putting their house in order is entirely up to them. Fisher insists, being alone is okay! Once aloneness is accepted, true togetherness is possible, but not before. What often masquerades as togetherness is collective indifference. Chaos, he asserts, gives way to order one person at a time. Once the choice is made workers can build towards a more rational ordering society.

Dr. Fisher's books probe the effect of big passions on small people, for he considers himself one of the small people. Born on the proverbial "wrong side of the tracks," this Phi Beta Kappa graduate of the University of Iowa, argues that he has seen "the haves" take his world, turn it upside down and make a shambles of it. He has no intention of mouthing pleasantries over this fact, not with management as he demonstrated in *Work Without Managers* (1991), nor with the working man or woman as he proves in this spellbinding book.

Dr. Fisher has worked for, observed, and been consultant to American and international concerns for the past thirty years. He is a former international corporate executive of Nalco Chemical Company and Honeywell, Inc., working in North and South America, Europe and South Africa. Fisher holds a doctorate in organizational and industrial psychology, and resides in Tampa, Florida with his wife, Betty, where he continues to write and consult.

—**Dr. Billy G. Gunter,** Emeritus Professor of Sociology, University of South Florida

NEED FOR CLEAR THINKING

"Almost all the opinions we have are taken by authority and upon credit."
—**Michel Montaigne,** French Renaissance philosopher

"Human beings can tolerate only a limited exposure to reality."
—**T. S. Eliot,** American-born British poet

THERE IS a long standing belief that the mentally healthy are more likely to have a deficient perception of reality than depressives. Depressives, so the argument goes, are better informed about their poor standing in the eyes of others than the healthy-minded. As they become less depressed, however, they discern an illusory increase in popularity. As you shall see, I hold little confidence with this argument. On the contrary, I feel the worker's survival is predicated on embracing reality, not denying it; on riding reality like the bull that it is until tempered to the worker's purposes.

Not a popular view, it demands *"going against the grain"* of venerated beliefs. This prompted someone to suggest that I am "the historian of despair and chronicler of sorrow." I earned this dubious distinction for my obtrusive observation of the complex organization naked, and for my failure to "pull my punches" in *Work Without Managers: A View from the Trenches* (1991). Perhaps more accurately it might be said **I** attempt to probe the effects of the big passions on us as persons, what sociologist Erving Goffman calls, *The Presentation of Self in Everyday Life* (1959).

Therefore, I have no intention of mouthing pleasantries, not with management, nor with the working man and woman. What I desire from the reader is to think and decide whether I make sense or not, with the emphasis on that rarest of intellectual enterprises, thinking, and using it to embrace, not deny reality.

From my perspective, the world is on a collision course between reality and the denial of that reality. Sheer population figures suggest that we must find a better way to work, relate and to calibrate experience. The current world population is more than seven billion souls. By the year 2050, it is projected to explode to more than 12.5 billion souls. Today most workers of the world live at or below the poverty level. How does this augur for future generations? Why?

What we are doing is not working anymore. Rhetoric won't solve our dilemma, nor will self-deception. Rhetoric expresses a geopolitical style of those who would deny the past, fear the future, and be self-conscious of the present. Our only salvation, it seems to me, is for workers everywhere to grasp the leadership baton, not wrench it from the hand of leadership, but gently reposition it on a more common sense course. Leadership seems hopelessly mired in a mental fog, lock stepping to the tyranny of expediency.

Clear thinking workers with a deep sense of duty can lift this fog and put society back on course. Such workers live in the embrace of trust, and are not afraid to differ, take risks or endure failure. These workers epitomize all that is good about being human. They are mature. They are adult. They are not suspended in permanent adolescence waiting for "orders from headquarters," but fully accepting responsibility for their own destiny and all the agony and ecstasy that destiny might entail.

—**James R. Fisher, Jr., Ph.D.**, Tampa, Florida

THE FEMININE PARADIGM

THE VELVET GLOVE

AN UPSIDE DOWN WORLD!

"Two extravagances: to exclude Reason, to admit only Reason."

—**Blaise Pascal,** French mathematician

ENGLISH POET John Donne (1572 – 1631) was wrong; Everyman today is an island unto himself, and his only redemption is in the realization and acceptance of that fact. The answers are not in government, nor industry and commerce, no longer in religion, and certainly not in science. So, you ask, "Where does that leave the worker?" I reply, "Very much alone!"

The expedience of naiveté does not improve the worker's longed for identity and recognition, nor does naiveté ensure the continuance of freedom, which is virtually taken for granted. The worker is on his own nickel, and there is no savior, no god, and no protector to shield him from the crush of history, from the inevitable force of reality, other than himself or herself.

What is missing is a lack of attention to fear. Workers are afraid to lead fuller lives, not because they embrace fear, but because they deny it by preoccupation with distractions. I understand fear. Fear runs through my body the way sap runs through a tree. I am attentive to fear each day of my life, for that day may be my last. Were I not so attentive I might be distracted and go to my grave without expressing these sentiments. Fear is a powerful positive in my life. It keeps me attentive. It finds me taking life seriously, but not myself.

By embracing my fear rather than retreating from it, I have an opportunity to soar over my misgivings and personal limitations to confidence in myself. This recognizes that answers to what troubles me are never "out there," but instead exist within my temperament, experience and capacity to flush them out and see them for what they are. Fear alerts the mind to pending danger. Henry Ward Beecher called it *"the soul's signal for rallying to the challenge."*

The working world is upside down. Cataclysmic change followed Johannes Gutenberg's (1395-1468) invention of the movable type printing press in 1450. First it was the Protestant Reformation in 1517, followed by the rise of national states across Europe, as well as the American and French Revolution nearly 250 years ago.

Similar cataclysmic change has been compressed in the past thirty years with the creation of the *Information Age* and all its electronic wizardry. Is it any wonder our world is upside down? That said what is seemingly complicating our dealing with change in particular and the working world in general is too much *HYPE*, too much dependence on Harvard, Yale and Princeton Elitism in law, politics, government, commerce, religion and industry. The consequence is that *HYPE* makes surreal demands on its competency, demands it cannot fulfill disguising its limitations in hubris and bravado.

These academic institutions have become veritable factories of inflated grading and solipsistic egos with graduates moving into politics and government, Wall Street and corporate boardrooms, academic and religious conclaves. There they have exercised infallible authority, and engaged in "business as usual" practices no matter how inappropriate. None of this, however, touches society's sick soul. We now have the benefit of hindsight seeing that some thirty years later little has changed with the exception that these institutions still remain essentially in control of our collective forward inertia.

The societal portrait of Dorian Gray withers grotesque, but remains undiscovered, hidden in the attic of our unconscious denying minds. Meanwhile, society, as collective individualism, stubbornly refuses to grow up, determined to remain indulgently suspended in adolescence. There are few mature adults in charge, only patriarchal parents. Society goes from child to parent, parent to child, only to skip the adult phase. Society is waiting for someone to "take charge," but no one is conditioned for such responsibility, so everyone suffers, especially the rank and file worker.

More evidence that people of this planet, not only the United States, live in an upside down world is that in 2014 the *British Oxfam International Humanitarian Group* reported that the 85 richest people in the world equaled the wealth of the bottom half of the global population. Stated another way, about 3.5 billion people, or half the world's population account for about $1.7 trillion, or about 0.7 percent of the world's wealth. Some $1.7 trillion happens to be the same amount attributed to the world's 85 richest people.

Nobel laureate (2001) in Economics Joseph E. Stiglitz argues in *"The Price of Inequality"* (2013) that America currently has the most inequality, and the least equality of opportunity among the advanced countries. While market forces play a role in this stark picture, politics has shaped those market forces.

In this book, Stiglitz exposes the efforts of well-heeled interests to compound their wealth in ways that have stifled true, dynamic capitalism. Along the way he examines the effect of inequality on our economy, our democracy, and our system of justice, while explaining how inequality affects and is affected by every aspect of national policy, and offers a vision for a more just and prosperous future, supported by a concrete program to achieve that vision.

He claims that while Congress reduced the taxes on the super rich and deregulated corporate operations in the 1980s to enlarge the economic pie, hoping that the middle class and those at the bottom would benefit, what has happened is that now the top 1 percent actually controls 40 percent of the nation's wealth.

This patriarchal society, where wealth and power reside in the privileged few, has denied repeatedly of being anachronistic as empires, emperors and despots have been relegated to the past. Feebly, in 2011, a movement developed which called itself "Occupy Wall Street" with the slogan "We are the 99%." This referred to income inequality in particular, and affluence inequality in general in the United States. The movement got media attention, but ran out of steam by late 2013, and nothing changed. That said the "1%" is more a global than a national reality, as one percent of the world's population has amassed about 46 percent of the world's wealth, or $110 trillion. That is 65 times the total wealth of the bottom half of the world's population. This should give those of unrestrained affluence little comfort as revolutions have erupted on less obvious premises.

A patriarchal driven society pushes for morality, which is only a mindset of the time, not a definitive proposition. While parents push for "what should be," children escape into impulsive pleasure. Parents, mystified by their collective ineptitude, abandon their values and join their children in "joy-living" distracting aberrations. It is the world of everything, anything, now!

In contrast mature adults display the patience and grit to deal with "what is," holding firmly to what makes sense and remains relevant. Unrestrained existence has become a legacy of capitalism not only existentially in economic terms but in behavior terms as well. Social justice is the perennial mantra, but clearly not the outcome.

With a disturbing absence of mature adults, polite chicanery is the order of the day, especially in the workplace. Appearances justify everything. Looking good eclipses doing good. This is very Socratic, for Socrates reduces philosophy essentially to a matter of manners, or refinement. He argues that the greatest wisdom, and best differentiation between good and evil is displayed in appearances. Well, *HYPE* exudes good manners. People of refinement hold their forks correctly, use earthy expletives only in polite company, and find their vocation as courtiers to power, metaphorically eating cake while a good share of the world's population has little access to bread. For the past half-century, those in charge have been promulgating Teflon means to justify synthetic ends, and workers everywhere have done nothing. Yet the fault lies not with *HYPE,* but with the workers, workers who sought sanctuary as if children from cradle to grave.

Whatever the enticement, the response of workers-as-children is always the same. Take the newest craze, information technology. The panacea of the atomic age, with its promise of cheap energy, now gives way to the *Information Age.* Workers have been persuaded that the logic of science translates into ever-expanding economic opportunity. Conveniently forgotten is the fact that nuclear power creates a waste that is impossible to destroy; that nuclear power has already upset the ecological balance of our planet, due in no small measure to society's collective ignorance of nuclear fallout.

Now, the blitzkrieg of information technology invades the defenseless mind and social fabric, encountering little skepticism. With modems and Internet software, the virtual community is a reality. Workers no longer have to sit in front of television screens and watch program patterns as they did in the 1950s. Workers now have the pacifier of their mobiles to talk dirty to the world. The virtual community, of the Internet has replaced physical and psychological intimacy, reducing behavior to confinement to a monitor screen, some electronic device, which is the equivalent of self-imposed solitary confinement. It is not only economic wealth that has turned the world upside down, but information technology has turned a wonderful new toolbox into an escape *"Toy of the Mind"* to anesthetized the individual from the growing breach between the haves and have nots.

Pop artist, Andy Warhol:

"When I got my first television set, I stopped caring so much about having close relationships."

Now, children as young as two or three have their own electronic pads to play games from sun up to sun down, only to look up to eat when they are hungry Warhol didn't live to see this implausible perversion of human relations. In a world of some seven billion souls, more than half of whom lack this luxury, they remain invisible to people in advanced industrial societies. These people fail to see themselves or each other as they, too, have their heads down texting, tweeting or exploring apps on laptops or smartphones. No one seems to appreciate the absurdity.

Incredibly, information technology displaces many workers from jobs and turns potentially skilled workers into low-level computer technicians. Computers may facilitate the work of scholars, scientists, engineers and writers, but computers also turn them into essentially typists. Yet from this most articulate, gifted and intellectually elite community, one hears nary a complaint.

SILENT INVASIONS!

> *W man of clear ideas errs grievously if he imagines that whatever is seen confusedly does not exist; it belongs to him, when he meets with such a thing to dispel the mist, and fix the outlines of the vague form which is looming through it."*
>
> —**John Stuart Mill,** English philosopher

WE LIVE IN a world of invasions. Countries invade other countries without provocation, governments invade our bedrooms as they attempt to legislate morality, men invade women as if it is their right, television invades our homes and minds to create a wasteland of purpose, obscenity as art invades our culture forsaking its role of promoting the nobility of man, and information technology invades all aspects of our private lives so that everything once sacred is now profane.

Now we also have electronic drone predators, pilotless small devices with cameras that can be controlled remotely and invade our every action. What's more, these devices can be armed with bullets or missiles to become killing machines as they have been used in Afghanistan and other troubled places in the world.

Police and the military have made George Orwell's *Nineteen Eighty-Four* (1949) a haunting reality.

Conceivably, to invade each other's privacy is the basic way perhaps the only way workers can relate to each other. There is little intimacy. The void created by its lack is now replaced by licentious gossip.

Supportive of this is daytime television, which thrives on invasion. It celebrates the most bizarre deviancies as common fare, while workers take "time out" from their banal lives to devour absurd exhibitionism without a whimper of protest. It is apparent by the ratings these programs generate that the audience delights in self-negation, self-degradation, for every person so exposed, violates everyone. What redeeming value does such exposure have for the human soul?

Moreover, as a society, workers tolerate an extraordinary amount of intrusive noise. They accept Muzak in shopping malls and airports, boom boxes on the street, television surveillance in banks and department stores. The electronic eye follows them everywhere, or subliminal aural stimulation attacks their subconscious. To an incredible degree, workers relish intrusion, especially media intrusion. They live vicariously through the personal lives and foibles of celebrities. Their own lives are so dull and boring to them that they may spend hours, which can literally grow into days, glued to their television screens following the lurid carnival of sex, crime and mayhem of certain celebrity personalities. Gossip is more grist for the mill than personal intimacy, while noise is a welcomed relief from intimidating silence.

Saul Bellows, Nobel Laureate in Literature (1976) in an essay published in 1975 called "Starting Out in Chicago," is most emphatic. He writes:

> *The enemy is noise. By noise, I mean not simply the noise of technology, the noise of money, or advertising and promotion, the noise of the media, the noise of miseducation, but the terrible excitement and distraction generated by the crisis of modern life.*

> *Mind, I don't say that philistinism is gone. It is not. It has found many disguises, some highly artistic and peculiarly insidious. But the noise of life is the great threat...*
>
> *The sound of the publish sphere, the din of politics, the turbulence and agitation that set in about 1914 and have now reached an intolerable volume.*

In a Tel Aviv speech, he asks the question:

> *How do you overcome noise? I don't really know whether art can exist without a certain degree of tranquility or spiritual poise; without a certain amount of quiet you can have neither philosophy nor religion nor painting nor poetry.*
>
> *And as one of the specialties of modern life is to abolish this quiet, we are in danger of losing our arts altogether with the quiet of the soul that art demands.*

Clearly, the quiet of intimacy has become increasingly taboo. It is too personal. Preferred is the scandalous, like sleeping around, or playing with that fantasy. This represents the reduction of behavior to instinct in order to fill a painful void. This is far less sinful than simply a waste.

DEUS EX MACHINA

As disturbing as the radicalism of the 1970s were in terms of abandoning our psychosexual mores, four decades later with the advent of the personal computer (PC), we have essentially forsaken our conscious self and undergone an evolutionary shift.

Computers, after all, are capable of simulating mental as well as physical activities. Not least of which is that anyone with an

34

iPhone knows he has speech conversion capability that reduces the boundaries between people and machines.

We are endanger of losing our humanity to robotics to become indistinguishable from our gadgets. Small wonder there is increasing anxiety and trouble in personal relationships between people.

So many of us are "in love" with our devices, unable to put them down during dinner, in a college lecture class, during a church sermon or television drama, glued to the TV screen of all sizes and shapes, all colors and embroidery, endlessly distracted by electronic pings, vibrations and buzzing.

This is the latest incarnation of a people who no longer find solace in God or the Christian Myth or that of any other religion.

Machines are no longer interchangeable, but it is people who are. Their identity has been high jacked by the machine. It is now the machine that has all the gravitas and personality. It is the machine that has become the new god.

Humans think and dream. They love. Love requires intimacy. Without love, there is no intimacy. Intimacy is quite possible without being sexual, but intimacy is absolutely a disaster when sexual without being intimate. Intimacy is synergistic. Its total emotional effect is greater than the sum of its parts. Conversely, promiscuity is consuming. Its emotional impact is to leave both parties exhausted, empty and despairing.

Despite this, workers hold to taboos against intimacy, the same way they cower from fear. Love is a four letter word with which most workers are uncomfortable. Yet love is the sinew missing from the muscle of today's organization: love of work, life, friendship, and being useful. Lust, greed and pleasure are the void fillers for those afraid of love.

Now, it is not lust but our gadgets that have intervened. Yet, the real test of human identity turns out not to be our current gadget obsession of the moment, but to be love.

Love conquers all. It is the one thing that is free, not for sale, but so difficult to find in our postmodern world.

Young people today, the new millennials, don't buy into any particular mindset. When young people suffer life a little, they crave intimacy. They move toward, not away from doubt. Being good lovers is not a primary quest. That is what their parents think and fear. Why? Because parents attempt to save their loveless marriages with sex. Millennials tend to take life and nature in stride with love, sex, and life as part of that nature.

Young people are driven by a need for identity and recognition. This is the motor of existence. They don't feel a need to rush nature. They can afford to let nature take its course. On the other hand, a common invention of parents is "perversion by example." Parental sexual conduct contaminates and invades the sanctuary of their youngsters. Were parents to behave differently, the behavior of their children would follow.

To take nature in stride is discarded by workers. Think of this a moment. Clocks are speeded up. Everyone is in a mad rush to go somewhere, which too often is nowhere, with no idea why. Workers are so busy getting nowhere that they have no time to take inventory of their personal lives. As a result, what should be important is mainly relegated to an afterthought. Life experience is an atavistic gesture which requires toys of distraction to fill the punishing void.

Psychologist Dr. Larry Kubiak has observed: *"Parents of teenagers spend an average of only 14 minutes each day communicating with their children. Only one minute is positive communication, and one minute is neutral. A whopping 12 minutes are negative."*

Many need to cry out in the void of their emptiness to authenticate themselves. The more embarrassing the circumstances the more they feel validated. This finds many compelled to "go public" with the most intimate details of their personal lives. Daytime television was made for them. Here talk show hosts raise humanity from the barbaric to the banal. Viewers privately scoff at this public display of disgrace. But who is the greater philistine —the exhibitionist or the voyeur? The more graphic and blatant the confessions the better. Such programming defines a society which has lost its center and moral compass.

Exhibitionism as therapy has become legitimate business. It is the main doctrine of Alcoholics Anonymous (AA). Alcoholics, who leave this high church and attempt to maintain their sobriety on their own, are called "dry drunks." Disclosure (and attendance at meetings), AA insists, is key to rehabilitation. Many other addiction centers say, "Amen!" Disclosure as therapy is used for smokers, gamblers, overeaters, spouse abusers, and the list goes on. Invasion of the personal domain is axiomatic as ends justify means. Privacy is suspended for cathartic relief as the cry reverberates, "Let it all hang out!"

What seems implicit in this expression is that workers don't know who or what they are. They need someone to tell them. They are desperate for approval from others so they may approve of themselves. Workers are in a virtual struggle for identity and recognition, for being reborn with a fresh sense of self.

Their historic dependence on management, or people in authority has eroded. Their counter dependency on the workplace has been torn asunder as many find themselves displaced persons, forced out of their jobs... ten, fifteen or twenty years before retirement age... and like Joseph K. in Franz Kafka's compelling novel, *The Trial (1925), "without having done anything wrong."*

Before, they took the boss's word as gospel, and the job as a certain thing. Now, that is all gone. They are alone, on their own, and they have never been taught to think and behave as mature adults. So, many escape into vices, vices which drive them to despair, with despair driving them to disclosure... "And the beat goes on."

As children, the focus of existence was on becoming somebody, not on being involved and committed to something now; on the competitive drive, not the spirit of cooperation; on the illusion of progress, not on the reality of experience.

But alas, thanks to decades of corrupt and incompetent leadership in all institutions, the squandering of natural resources, the impatience of youth and discriminated minorities, the persistence of psychological and physiological abuse, burgeoning chaos and violence, the dream has died. In so doing workers are now forced to embrace despair. Despair is the only cure for illusion. Without the penetrating pain of despair, workers fail to grow up. In the end time runs out on suspended adolescence, the dominant state of workers in the past century and now as well in the 21st century. The youth must die to give birth to the mature adult. It is a painfully slow and agonizing process, but inevitable.

The pain of reality drives workers now to an ever-expanding consciousness. This goes beyond seeking rational economic parity. Workers demand more, not less, control of their lives at all levels: spiritual, intellectual, emotional, economic and political. They have had it. They find they can trust no one but themselves. This new found sense of self can only lead to the collapse of tyranny in the workplace—the tyranny generated by comfort, by the patronizing paternalism of omniscient and benevolent management.

A pat on the head will no longer suffice. Workers want their power back. But before this will occur, human nature will take a circuitous route to this objective, a senseless but inevitable escape into regression. Novelist George Orwell states this in general terms: *"The choice for mankind lies between freedom and happiness and for the great bulk of mankind, happiness is better."* Those in power know and exploit this preference.

This is where we find workers today. "Want" has become need; legitimate tools, toys. Computers, iPads, laptops, smartphones or the yet-to-be invented new widget they believe will satisfy that want and provide that freedom, as well as happiness. And so, these tantalizing distractions are embraced in a quest of delusional "empowerment and liberation."

When sophisticated legitimate tools become toys of distraction, the illusion is created that workers are "expanding individual choice and demonstrating freedom." What these workers fail to understand is that they are escaping into Toyland. At this writing, many middle class workers are slaves to call waiting, e-mail, text messages, tweets, the Internet or their video cell phones—acting out their roles as historical caricatures of the times.

Jayson Demers of AudienceBloom reports an overwhelming proportion of workers say they spend a significant portion of the work day on *non-work work.*

Today's worker is tempted by a bevy of distractions to wander off to the cafeteria for a coffee, sit at his workstation and check his messages, surfing the Internet, playing a game on apps, looking at the latest pictures of his friends on Facebook, or other postings, resuming his work only to interrupt that by responding to a new voice mail, tweet or text message.

If not that, the worker is drowning in personal and work related e-mails, or having to attend pointless meetings routinely and ritualistically scheduled without a meaningful agenda or purpose related to his job or work related outcomes.

Rather than adapting to the electronic heavy world we now live in, employees are being pulled away more than ever from productive work.

In its annual "Wasting Time at Work Survey," Salary.com reported that 89 percent of respondents admitted to wasting time at work each day.

Some admitted they wasted as much as half of an eight our workday on *non-work, or on activities of a personal nature.*

The median weekly wage for workers in the US in 2015 was $786. Are employers getting what they're paying for? The odds are stacked against them. A Gallup study found that only 30 percent of the American workforce is engaged. The rest is costing companies up to $550 billion annually.

Whether employers know it or not, they are probably paying their employees to socialize with coworkers, to make personal phone calls, and to text and tweet with friends, and even shop on-line.

Check out the study of *Salary.com,* which reveals that pretty much everything there is to know about wasting time at work.

If you value productivity and performance, whether employer or employee, prepare to be shocked by what that survey found out.

Given this assessment, it might even be concluded that work is actually designed to waste time in the workplace with an implicit agreement between workers and managers for these silent invasions.

The history of workers is not revealed in causes, nor silent invasions. History presents only a blank succession of unexplained events. Society's *historical persona,* as it is normally written, usually represents public events which hyphenate technical achievements. Meanwhile, spiritual or inner events, which are most real, and what life is all about, are largely ignored or forgotten.

Life is meant to be lived, moment to moment, not explained or justified. Only unconscious activity bears fruit. Workers, who play a part in their times, never understand their true significance. Should they attempt to understand them, as the politically correct would have them act, they are struck with sterility.

The bleak truth is the more workers condone silent invasion the less authentic they become to themselves. Invasion has come to represent the social machinery for concealing the spectacle of human impotence and irrelevance and blindness—the ordinary details of daily existence.

Most observers mistake the outer accidents of existence, events which lie outside the worker's soul—social, economic, and political realities—for that which alone is genuine, the reality of experience.

British philosopher Isaiah Berlin writes:

> *"... the individual experience, the specific relation of individuals to one another, the colors, smells, tastes, sounds and movements, the jealousies, loves, hatreds, passions, the rare flashes of insight, the transforming moments, the ordinary day-to-day success of private data... constitute all there is."*

Technology as gimmick is widespread, exposing joyless materialism, lonely crowds, complacent consumerism, and an anthill culture in a homogenized meatloaf era. Everything is meant to be gulp down, not tasted. Culture is inauthentic; too many paperbacks, too little creativity. Ubiquitous technology narrows and isolates consumers into more minuscule pigeonholes of tastes to be targeted for exploitation. This is another silent invasion of privacy. Yet, the invasion is not denounced, but applauded. Workers celebrate the compelling distraction of technology from reality. What feeds the mind is not necessarily food for the soul.

This silent invasion has taken on the characteristics of paranoia since September 11, 2001, when Al-Qaeda terrorists used commercial jetliners as missiles and destroyed the Twin Towers in New York City, killing nearly 3,000 innocent people at work in these towers. The 2003 preemptive invasion of Iraq followed justified with the CIA intelligence that Iraq had weapons of mass destruction (WMDs), which proved not to be the case. Thereafter, the vigor of surveillance by the Central Intelligence Agency (CIA) and National Security Agency (NSA) intensified, not only in combat zones and across the United States, but globally as well. George Orwell's "Big Brother" was now the maniacal focus of the world.

Three young men of no compelling distinction became prominent as whistle blowers, or as some would describe them as "traitors." Whatever the designation or their motivation, they were in a position to leak "secrets" that were called by some "against national security," and by others simply national embarrassments.

Edward Snowden, Bradley Manning and Julian Assange, now famous or infamous for their acts, are in isolation at this writing, one in hiding, one in a foreign embassy, and one in prison.

Manning released to Assange's website, WikiLeaks, some 720,000 secret documents from the State and Defense Departments, and Assange published them on the Internet. These documents contain some of the US's most closely guarded secret surveillance programs.

Snowden, a CIA computer analyst, disclosed top secret NSA documents to several media outlets revealing details of global

NSA surveillance, including the e-mails of some of the US's most trusted allies, including Germany's Chancellor Angela Merkel.

Professor David Cole of Georgetown University writes soberly:

"While we as members of the public have learned from each of these men about what our government has done behind closed doors in our name, they have also taken it upon themselves to reveal hundreds of thousands of secret documents, only some of which may have been just flabbily disclosed. No one elected Snowden, Manning, or Assange to act as our conscience. But if they didn't so act, who would?" (New York Review, February 6, 2014).

THE PRICE OF INNOCENCE!

"In our time, what is at issue is the very nature of man, the image we have of his limits and possibilities as man. History is not yet done with its explanation of the limits and meaning of human nature."

—**C. Wright Mills,** American sociologist

TECHNOLOGY IS a whirling dervish. No one has any idea where it will lead. Obviously it tampers with the mind and is observable every day and everywhere. Take the housewife I observed standing in line at the supermarket, as I waited to pay for my purchases. With her mobile in hand, she talked to herself leaving a text message to someone, then turned to me and laughed in my ear, "Isn't this crazy, but she'd kill me if I didn't get back to her right away!" Little did I know that day that this peculiar behavior would represent only the tip of the iceberg of what has become the norm.

It is hard to find anyone who isn't dipping their head to talk into their mobile to leave a text message, or moving their fingers quickly across the glass surface of the mobile to leave a text message or check out an app.

The blurring of the real and the imagined finds workers electronic junkies oblivious to their surroundings. Listening to this housewife put me in mind of a television "reality show" where cameras follow a family through every moment of their day, while millions watch these productions as if their own lives are not dramatic enough. Ironically, little do these viewers know how carefully crafted and orchestrated these shows are to register the greatest "soap opera" impact.

The world today is not a new-found absurdity as it was for Jean-

Paul Sartre and Albert Camus. It is a place where absurdity is the plausible norm and manages to sound, to all but the most satirical minds, like truth and reason. Indeed, today we are in George Orwell's world of "doublethink," where we have the power of holding two contradictory beliefs in our minds, simultaneously, and accepting both of them as true. Even using a smartphone or iPad like a toy is normal behavior, a triumph of technology. You don't have to ask your lymph nodes about it or become embarrassed if you walk into a wall, or the worst-case scenario, texting while going up the down ramp on the interstate. This has become a disturbing trend with many automotive casualties. If the trend continues, it will eclipse drunken driving as the main cause of vehicular fatalities.

Meanwhile, entire communities have become sink holes of despair, rife with crime, violence, illegitimacy, illiteracy, poverty, homelessness, disease and chaos.

Ambushed by free floating anxiety, workers have lost touch with touch. They are clowns in everyday dress. Hostile, perhaps even hateful for losing a job or being taken for granted, they strike out blindly at shadows. They adopt the tactics of their enemies — paranoia, gossip, innuendo, backstabbing, and blackballing. Whatever their inclination — homophobic, militant or racist — they become essentially their own worst enemy.

The obliging media unwittingly contributes to this deception as they position mirrors to capture "the best" glimpse of workers — strong, fearless, purposeful, alert, skillful, responsible, industrious. What these mirrors fail to capture is the real self, which is far less pretty, closer to the opposite — weak, fearful, ambivalent, lethargic, inept, irresponsible, and indolent. To no one's surprise workers insist on the image of themselves as hero to that of wimp.

Still, these mirrors reflect only the outer self, the guile of invention, not the inner self, the engine of the soul, which lies beyond the depth of mirrors. To wit:

Workers believe this the land of unlimited opportunity, even as opportunity disappears. When failures occur, blame is the game. At one level, failure is the nervous tic of the worker's lack of skill, initiative, greed or indifference. At another level, failure plays against the inept elements of society, which are judged to be distortions in "the system." Fix these aberrations and all will fall into place. Politicians happily play these nonsense strings and point their finger in every direction but at the problem. No one talks about a finite world, an increasingly crowded world, or a shrinking economic pie with limited opportunity. Instead, godlike, workers have been persuaded by these demigods of the Establishment that it is their destiny to remake the world into their "own image and likeness."

Workers embrace the warped vision of a new golden age. They tie their hopes and aspirations to a scientifically managed society which cures all social ills. All signs to the contrary are ignored. Optimism governs the rank and file worker, but she never governs wisely. No one is encouraged to ask the question: why the wealth and mind gap?

As mentioned earlier, economist Joseph Stiglitz first identified the problem *(Price of Inequality* 2013) and later proposed the solution *(The Great Divide: Unequal Societies and What We Can Do About Them,* 2015).

But alas, macroeconomic theory is not enough. It seldom if ever translates smoothly into microeconomics without "boots on the ground." That transition usually takes a social revolution. Is that where we are heading?

Workers see economic parity as their birthright. They see themselves with an ever-expanding share of the economic pie. It has never happened before, and it is unlikely to happen in the future. The proportionate distribution of resources has not changed dramatically since the 17th Century.

During the American Revolution, 40 percent of the wealth was controlled by 10 percent of the population. On the eve of the Civil

War, 70 percent of the nation's resources were still controlled by 10 percent of the people. Industrialization had an even more devastating effect on the distribution of resources. In the first decade of the 20th Century, 60 percent of the nation's wealth was controlled by 2 percent of the people, while the bottom 65 percent controlled but 5 percent of the wealth.

Since World War II, the top 20 percent has controlled 40 percent, while the bottom 40 percent controlled less than 6 percent. Although workers admittedly benefited with a generous slice of the economic pie immediately after WWII, between 1968 and 1981, real wages for the average worker declined 20 percent.

This trend has continued into the 21st century aggravated by tax shelters for the rich and deregulation. The economic pie grew for the wealth creators, but shrunk considerably for the middle class and working class; not at all the predicted or expected outcome.

The cushion of comfort, provided by post WWII demands, has disappeared. In 1947, United States workers produced 60 percent of the world's industrial goods. Today it is 30 percent. Manufactured goods, such as automobiles, agricultural machinery and telecommunications have declined as much as 30 to 50 percent. And there is little promise that the "information highway" will miraculously impact these statistics positively. In fact, as pointed out earlier, with 85 individuals controlling half of the global wealth, technology, if anything, has accelerated this economic divide.

Workers insist in the belief that they live in a classless society. Decreasing economic mobility, however, emphasizes class lines. Moreover, workers are tired, tired of social climbing, tired of explaining individual failure, or failure of national leadership. Tired as they are, they still cower from reality, seeking refuge under the canopy of denial. Workers cannot accept that the boom is over. Meanwhile, politicians exploit their ambivalence. Both political parties assure workers that the boom is not over. Both sound the same the same, the rhetoric is the same, the assumptions identical.

The common good, upon which the Republic was founded, now appears a radical idea as lobbyists in Congress skew legislation emanating from both parties towards special interests.

Polling controls the mind of government, and by extension, the minds of the governed. Workers fail to see how this sponsors and spawns leaderless leadership, or how it places their wellbeing in permanent jeopardy. Badly misled, workers have been conditioned to see the whole in terms of the part — mesmerized by their own special needs and requirements. Ethnocentrism is common to workers and politicians alike. Such an inclination brings out the *Renaissance Man* in some, the fascist in others. Workers are primed for fascism, for a quick fix to the overwhelming problems of crime, violence, economic turmoil and social unrest. Caught between two colossi, one of which has no heart and the other no head, they are primed for this as they gulp down tasteless food, sit indolently in freeze frame before their televisions or computers, listen to mechanical noise alluding to be music, or talk like automatons discussing automobiles (made in Japan) or electronics (made in Taiwan). Despite little evidential support, workers revel in the conviction they are still the greatest.

Workers favor computers in the classroom, the earlier the better. First graders have laptops, many even cell phones, if not smartphones. Yet eight, ten, or twelve years later, these same students cannot do their multiplication tables, long or short division, fractions, cannot balance a check book; don't know how to diagram a sentence; don't know a gerund from a participle; don't remotely know American—much less—world history; or cannot spell 200 common words, while reading at the dull normal level.

This is painfully illustrated as more than a million skilled workers are imported each year because students-as-workers are ill prepared. Technology promises to make for a more educated society, a society which will lead to a more harmonious and engaged workforce. The exact opposite is occurring as we become more technology friendly. Eminent futurists such as Arthur C. Clarke, James Martin, and Loy Singleton declare that hand-held electronic pocket tutors will revolutionize education worldwide. It sounds good, but learning is equally a social process as well as a mechanical function.

Even the notable psychologist, Carl Rogers, sees high-tech communications as the key to person-centered education. He hails it "the promise of a new dawn of enlightenment." Rogers predicts global competition will be replaced by cooperation, respect for others, and mutual helpfulness. History suggests otherwise. Human nature has changed little in recorded history. It is inclined to hoard, bully, exploit weakness, frustrate purpose, divide and conquer.

These prominent voices seem plagued with the same feeble myths workers crave to hear. Mythology as hope does not beget courage. It assumes a linear connection between the distribution of sophisticated technology and the manifestation of altered states of awareness, and more idyllic forms of human behavior. There is no substitute for love, and love is not likely to be found in printed wire circuit memory boards.

Workers confuse rights and privileges. For instance, a public school education is the privilege of citizenship. This gives the individual, whatever his circumstances, an opportunity to expand his consciousness and tap his inherent potential. Public school education is a remarkable privilege of modern society, which has little to do with rights. But treated as a right, however, it is sure to be abused. Students feel they are doing society a favor by becoming educated. So, they fight it. What we obtain too cheaply, we esteem too lightly.

When students complete twelve years of public education, at virtually no cost to them, and are unable to read or comprehend these words here, they have failed themselves. Blame it on "the system," ethnicity, family, or poverty, the fact remains the individual is ultimately responsible in this world for himself. The sense of this has been lost as rights are flaunted and privileges forgotten. It would seem the price of innocence is a form of intolerable complicity in the end.

LATE BLOOMING ROSES!

"Men are grown mechanical in head and heart, as well as hand. Their whole effort, attachments, opinions turn on Mechanism, and are of a mechanical character."

—**Thomas Carlyle,** Scottish philosopher

WORKERS ARE addicted to lingering dependence. Who is to blame? Is it culture? Can a capitalistic society of liberal democracy produce a stable workforce in which workers are satisfied? Is satisfaction an essential to economic solidarity? Does a democratically driven culture raise humanity only from barbarism to banality? Does such banality breed instability and spiritual deprivation?

Weighty questions. Many prefer to contemplate such questions as *"How many angels can dance on the head of a pin?"* As absurd as this question might seem, variations of it have been used many times as cunningly dismissive as medieval angelology or scholasticism.

The phrase has been used to criticize such philosophers as Duns Scotus and Thomas Aquinas. In modern usage, it has been used as metaphor for wasting time debating topics of no practical value, or questions whose answers hold no intellectual consequence, while more urgent concerns pile up.

Many promote this preoccupation because it is an idle and safe activity, and takes them off the hook. What workers of such a mind conveniently forget is that they are the culture! They are society! They are the company! It is not something "out there," but in their sinews, bones and blood and running through their veins.

We saw the clash of reality with idealism when President

Barack Obama's *Affordable HealthCare Act* of universal health coverage was finally implemented. Senators and Congressmen and Congresswomen of the president's Democratic Party abandoned him, insurance companies grew anxious, Wall Street became cynical, and the public retreated into confusion as it tried to sign up on the HealthCare.gov home page of the Internet in late 2013 and early 2014.

The roles and relationship of leaders with followers have changed in this burgeoning electronic age. It is no longer the parent to the accommodating child, no longer the manager to the submissive worker. Society has evolved to an adult interdependent role and relational context that has not yet reached fruition. Consequently, the trauma is understandable as is the metaphor appropriate of the late blooming rose.

This is being written as the Affordable HealthCare Act is now the law of the land. People are using this new universal medical care system—and ironies of ironies—both Democrats and Republicans are in support of it, for it is now part of our culture as is FICA (Federal Insurance Contributions Act), better known as the Social Security System. No politician dare vote against social security. Now politicians are saddled with the same reality with Obamacare.

Workers can no longer play dumb or wax innocent. They have no one to blame for the present societal malaise, but themselves. They have not been deprived of outlets to strive for mastery of themselves. The plunge into chaos has been a gratuitous retreat. Instead of changing their ways, instead of taking matters into their own hands and doing something about the situation, workers have allowed themselves to be treated as interchangeable parts, and to perfect the pathetic role of victim of circumstances. Massive redundancy exercises in which tens of thousands of highly skilled workers have lost their jobs, represents a single factor — a lack of attentiveness.

Likewise, the rollout of Obamacare, while the focus was on the president, the initial delivery glitch was as much a failure of the titans of the computer software industry as bureaucrats in the Obama Administration, not to mention the passivity of institutional authority in general and individual engagement in particular. The days of waiting for orders from headquarters have been committed to history.

Since the days of Isaac Newton, heads and hearts have been like parts to a finely tuned watch. Workers since Newton have been conditioned to think of themselves as parts of that machine, mechanized to be controlled not only in the material aspects of society, but through philosophy, art, literature, and music. No surprise, workers are consumed with mechanistic obsessions. All efforts, all attachments, opinions, turn on mechanisms, even redemption (Deliverance) is of a mechanistic nature.

Souls of steel provide little solace to pristine innocence. Sinclair Lewis in his 1920 classic, *Main Street,* saw how oppressive standardization was killing the moral fiber of the community, and by extension, its spirit:

> *"It is contentment... the contentment of the quiet dead. . . it is slavery self-sought and self-defended. It is dullness made God... A savorless people, gulping tasteless food, and sitting afterward, coatless and thoughtless, in rocking chairs prickly with inane decorations, listening to mechanical music, saying mechanical things about the excellence of Ford automobiles, and viewing themselves as the greatest race in the world."*

The primacy of workers is to fulfill their needs through a rational economic process. This finds them selling themselves and their integrity to the highest bidder. The ethics of this proposition never comes to mind.

But alas, economics have not been enough. Being well-heeled financially has not brought workers physical health or spiritual happiness. It has led instead to a state of panic, *The Prison of Panic called "Now!"* Workers behave as if the boom will last forever, while fearing it won't. *"Power is tearing minds to pieces,"* George Orwell writes in his novel, 1984, *"and putting them together again in new shapes of your own choosing."*

A cursory review suggests that for the past half century comfort and entitlements have been exchanged for power and control. What was thrown in by the workers, "free of charge," was their identity and individual recognition. Workers couldn't or wouldn't see past their noses. Short-term gain was the focus at the expense of long-term consequences. Workers trusted their employers and management — nothing wrong with that! What workers didn't expect, or consider, because they didn't pay attention, is that what goes up must come down, for this is what happens to a society as it moves along the continuum from boom to bust. Now, many workers are powerless, millions jobless. They epitomize "the victim."

Anything as important as work cuts to the core of the human soul. Without work, there is little sense of self. Without work, it is an embarrassment to breathe. Society is driven by the pervasive theme, "He who works has clout and rules the roost." Mere reflection on this reminds workers how inattentive they have been. How they have tricked themselves.

Like Goethe's *Faust*, workers have sold their soul, and now wish to buy it back at bargain basement prices. The current obsession with identity and recognition is nothing less than a consuming drive to get a second chance. This is the engine of an eventual societal revolution.

Seduced by the dollar, workers participate in a painful irony. They are always paid a dollar more an hour than they can afford to quit. This keeps a lid on their lips, their obliging spirits in a cage, and finds them forever fearful of taking control of their lives.

Workers everywhere know it is dangerous to see clearly that the company is going in the wrong direction, and to express it openly to management, a management that operates with infallible authority and insists on business as usual practices even when such practices are counterproductive. Places of employment are often led by wrongheaded managers who could profit by listening to their workers. Failure of workers to have a distinct voice in operations penalizes employers and workers alike. Everybody loses. All because the almighty dollar blinds workers into fainthearted submissiveness.

So what do workers do? If they don't challenge the boss when things are wrong, how is their anger and frustration expressed? It is expressed in a cornucopia of grief. Workers whine about their plight to each other, sabotage operations, take bogus sick leave, participate in work slowdowns, and become passive personalities, as if the job were a separate entity, apart from themselves. Few, if any, consider going against the grain and launching a constructive counterattack.

Nearly a trillion dollars is lost each year from worker self-betrayal, which is still defended with the motto, *"Get as much as you can, while the getting is good! Stick it to them before they stick it to you!"* Lost in this incredible confusion is that workers, themselves, are the company! They are robbing themselves, killing their own possibilities. Individuals are society! The system and the government, likewise, are not separate from citizens, but integral to them. In a democratic society, they are in charge. It is the fault of no one but themselves for their failure to act responsibly.

A conspiracy of silence denies this. Even the most dedicated workers refuse to worry about, much less snitch on laggards, pilferers and saboteurs, or to concern themselves about cash-flow problems, profit & loss statements, expanding or contracting markets, cost of materials, or the reliability of design, because *"That is not my job! "This* is outside the purview of their concerns, as industries, plants, markets and jobs disappear, or collapse and die. Selective naiveté does not beget security for anyone.

Managers are employees, too, no more owners than workers. True, managers traditionally assume the role of surrogate owner, and comport themselves as if it is "their company." This is an accidental invention triggered by the abandonment of power and control by workers.

Management is a relatively new profession, which has grown out of two World Wars in the 20th Century. Workers, with little forethought, empowered management to be their conscience, caretaker, benefactor and protector. Workers, in a word, gave up control of their lives for comfort. For fifty years now, workers have luxuriated in a climate of sublime comfort and complaisant dependence.

Now, workers want their power back, but without risk, pain or consequence. They want their cake and eat it, too. But what is given away can seldom be returned. This is especially true of power. That is why there are all these "fun and games" about empowerment, when, in fact, no power is given back, not one iota of it.

If power is to be regained, there will be the spilling of real blood. There will be struggle and sacrifice. Major League baseball players (indeed, all professional athletes) have Curt Flood to thank for their collective bargaining power. It cost Flood his career. Now, no one remembers him. Many workers will have to pay a similar price.

> At the end of the 1969 baseball season, the St. Louis Cardinals of the National League in Major League Baseball attempted to trade or swap several baseball players for several others, among them was Curtis Flood, an outstanding outfielder of the Cardinals. Flood refused to go.
>
> Not only did he refuse to go, but he went to his personal lawyer and then to Marvin Miller, founder and executive director of the Players Association, declaring he wanted to sue Major League Baseball.
>
> The decision sent shock waves not only through baseball, but ultimately through all professional sports. Those waves reverberate even to this day. Although aware of the possible costs to him career wise, he never wavered.
>
> Players up to that point were treated as if property of the owners, for life, with owners able to do with them whatever they chose to do. Flood changed that. He went *against the grain* and liberated players from being treated as chattel by owners. It essentially ended his career, but gave power back to players, which they have exercised to this day.

The whole empowerment movement is counterfeit. The sooner workers realize this the sooner they can adopt a strategy to recover what has been lost. Management has no intentions of giving up its power. It is content to play MONOPOLY with workers' lives, a game played with funny money, which buys nothing but delay.

In any case the workers are not ready. Power demands attributes missing in most modern workers — such attributes as accountability, grace under pressure, inclination to take risks, accept blame, endure failure, believe in themselves when no one else will, do their best even when no credit comes their way, and be driven more by an ideal than money.

Power demands other things as well. Should they be treated as chattel, as was the case with baseball player Curtis Flood, power demands that they go against the grain, hold their ground, and stand up for their rights under the law. There is a considerable difference between securing a paycheck every two weeks, and worrying twenty-four hours a day if the job gets done and within costs, on schedule, fully meeting all customer requirements. It is the difference between treating work as a job and as a career, which is an expression of the worker's soul.

If you say many managers don't pass this test, you would be correct. Managers are power brokers, not power barons. They must, as with workers, be kept happy, fully employed, with sufficient staff and resources. This is the burden of real power. Identity and recognition are related closely to where the buck stops, and is often far removed from where the work takes place.

To many workers, the future is an illusion with denial the hammer of indifference. They refuse to see the handwriting on the wall and so turn to consultants to read it to them. Consultants are problem simplifiers. That is their role. Anything that will suggest to workers that the situation is "not their fault," or can project blame elsewhere is destined to be a big seller. Blame the situation on inadequate tools, poor training, cheap foreign labor, gender and race discrimination, unfair labor practices, inequitable trade policies, poor management, the National Debt, anything but on workers, themselves, and you have a responsive audience and customer. The irony is that there may be some truth to this set of cherry-picked justifications, but they don't put workers in a stronger position of negotiation, nor indeed, do they get workers' power back.

The reason these deficiencies resonate is because they have some legitimacy. Yet, these deficiencies mask the real problem, which is full cooperation and synergistic commitment of everyone to the same goal. If everyone is on the same page, then everyone can get off on the same dime. To put this in even more pragmatic terms, plainspoken philosopher Eric Hoffer claims, with reason, that the dregs of society in skid row are capable of building a city if lifted from their embarrassment.

Consultants, specialists and writers attack the disorder

from the outside, as they must. They suggest reinventing or re-engineering the corporation, anything but asking workers to radicalize their thinking, or to challenge their effort to maximize their contribution.

By attacking the problem from the outside, these well-meaning experts inadvertently fabricate a new "we/they" polarity, and promote a new rendition of an old song, disenchantment. Cosmetic surgery, for that is what is likely to be proposed, fails to touch the worker's soul, which is his sense of ownership of what he does.

Take the current obsession with quality. At first cut, this looks commendable. Who can argue with the validity of quality or quality standards in the conduct of work? The problem is with the obsession with quality standards. This is where the fault lies. Lost in this pursuit is the need for increased production and greater product diversification, essential components to the creation of new jobs.

Quality and performance standards are mindsets, not specific ways of doing things—not the ABCs of this or that formula (W. Edwards Deming notwithstanding); this or that model or paradigm; this or that fad.

Obviously, a mindset is important. If workers don't believe in a good idea, it will fail. On the other hand, if they believe in a bad idea, it will succeed. With quality or performance standards, there is no attempt to radicalize the way workers think. The approach is totally mechanistic, simplistic and therefore ephemeral. Still, workers, like obedient children, go along with the drill, and play out the charade. Once again, expediency wins.

The-Worker-as-Thinker is a new idea, an idea left out of the equation, not only in the workplace but in all phases of society. Workers as thinkers are far removed from community involvement in the collapsing social order of crime, poverty, homelessness, homicide, suicide, genocide and moral decay. Nor are workers motivated to get involved. They prefer to sit in the bleachers of society and criticize it from afar. They love talk radio where they can ventilate their frustrations with anonymity and without consequences. Once again, "Not my problem!" But it is.

Order is first established inside the individual, one-person-at-a-time, before any behavioral change is manifested outside in society-at-large. Change the man from a passive person to an active personality with a social conscience, involved in the management and maintenance of society, and you change the world.

This demands more than simply the changing of the worker's mind. It requires the creation of a radically different mentality. Anything less is to fall victim to mechanistic pretense, or irritating aberrations which fail to touch anyone. It is the "Adult" and the "Reality Principle" in Freudian terms, as opposed to the "Parent" and the "Morality Principle," or the "Child" and the "Pleasure Principle."

Workers are compliant, amorphous, and like silly putty, can be molded into many forms. They may build castles of sand on psychic islands, drifting through life lost in a sea of confusion, or be programmed to obsessional levels regarding their physical well-being. Trigger words, such as "social security" and "universal health coverage," or "lifetime employment" and "eternal youth" can make them forget the spiritual foundation of their common humanity. These trigger words spell "comfort" and "security." Workers are ready to barter their souls for such satisfaction. "Getting" blocks out their natural inclination to "giving." Mention is made of Freud, who is a bit passé in current conversation, but he correctly anticipated how far workers would retreat from reality into comfort and complacency.

But mankind is a single entity, with every worker an essential part of a common fabric. Worker power, identity and recognition are not national issues, but global themes. If workers continue to be preoccupied with nonsense, with self-indulgent concerns, while allowing others to solve their problems, to make choices for them, then most employment is bound to be purposeless; bound to lead to an eternity of lingering dependence. It is time for workers, like late blooming roses, to come to grips with their situation. Otherwise, those workers made redundant will forever echo the tired refrain, *"How can this happen to me, when I have done nothing wrong?"* It is not a question of wrongdoing, but what have you done right?

LIFE WITHOUT A CAUSE!

"Arthur Schopenhauer points out that when you reach an advanced age and look back over your lifetime, it can seem to have had a consistent order and plan, as though composed by some novelist. Events that when they occurred had seemed accidental and of little moment turn out to have been indispensable factors in the composition of a consistent plot. So who composed the plot? Schopenhauer suggests that just as your dreams are composed by an aspect of yourself of which your consciousness is unaware, so, too, your whole life is composed by the will within you."

—**Joseph Campbell,**
American writer and mythologist

MATURE ADULT WORKERS know the universe has no cause. It exists. Most workers, however, insist on being driven by causes. True believers cannot function unless embroiled in some cause. It is the way they authenticate themselves.

The idea that the universe has no cause is overwhelming. "Why are we here, then?" cries everyman. Reality replies, "We are here because we exist." We come out of nature and return to nature. But most workers must believe there is more. They refuse to deal with nature "as is," feeling compelled to control it, no, even to conquer and change nature.

Man demonstrates his superiority by subduing nature to his will. But again and again, as he is so engaged, nature vanquishes him. For such blinding pride, workers are but strangers to themselves and occupants of a dying planet. The culprit is their obsession with control, the need to subdue what the mind encompasses. Thought creates a duality between "what is" and "what should be."

"What should be" moves the mind away from the problem of "what is" to a fixation with effects. This springs from a mishmash of causes. Man is forever terrified contemplating his own nature. He is hypersensitive, even hypocritical to what is most natural. Sexual pleasure has become a god, a ghost and a ghoul, depending on the orientation. Desire has given birth to consuming as therapy, while the issue of political correctness demonstrates the absurdity of sophistic causes.

Workers are not happy campers. They have come to take themselves too seriously, and life not seriously enough. A focus on effects cures nothing. It only invents new causes and gives birth to an army of experts and crusaders. In the past century, the popular mind, better known as the "crowd of discontent," created a new *Tower of Babel* in which language devolved into a litany of complaint.

Workers as "true believers" find a sense of belonging in a cause, a cause which is never their own. A mania for causes creates the world of the crazy, the confused and the moronic, the world of today. Ask yourself, "Who put workers in their cages?"

Reality can never be changed into morality, or "what is" into "what should be." Nor can anyone put order into someone else's life. To realize order, workers must do it themselves. This can be done by breaking free from the madness of the cage, and embracing the freedom of choosing one's destiny, not having it dictated.

So, what do most workers do? They ask for cages. They seek relief from the cage of workaholism, and the stress that it entails, for the cage of libidinous excess, or the cage of chemical dependency. Others not so inclined, seek relief from their anguish by having no life outside of work. The only uniform they wear is that of organizational counter dependency. The cage is their escape from freedom. It is home.

Many have come to find organized religions, and, indeed, major corporations as cages of false promises and suspect legitimacy, giving assurances that they cannot or will not keep. While churches claim to embody truth and the road to spiritual salvation, corporations claim the pathway to economic security and personal identity.

Psychologically, these promises, implied or inferred are based upon trust, which is the most powerful of weapons.

There is nothing we want so much as reassurance that we are on the right track and in the right place.

Most religions offer this in absolute terms while corporations present it in relative terms in their recruiting literature. The workforce today is better educated than ever before. It accumulates special knowledge always careful to express and behave within accepted norms. Nothing is original. The workforce is stuck on the dime and therefore society along with it.

This finds workers confused, uncertain, stressed, driven from one anxiety to another, until the point is reached where they cannot think, feel or act alone. They are terrified of a room without noise, a space without people, or a single moment when the mind is quiet. They are spastic, yet incredibly, this seems to be the norm.

A mind caught up in knowledge as a means to freedom does not become free. It becomes enslaved to knowing. The more information it has the more it must have. A worker in trouble feels he needs another degree, another seminar, another shot of inspiration from the master, the person with all the answers, who, like his religious predecessor, is unlikely to have spent much time doing in the real world.

Workers have created the mystique which suggests they are not capable of taking care of themselves. Thus is born the syndrome of dependency:

In the workplace: The dependency is on the manager for direction and control, or counter dependency on the organization for security, identity and recognition.

At home: It is dependency on elaborate social outreach programs of the government meant to compensate for the disappearance of a family centered culture. The majority of families seldom share a daily meal together, the round table of a family centered culture. The government now owns the problem, a problem which it can never solve.

In school: The dependency is on teachers and school administrators to assume a responsibility that is a privilege granted to the student for greater mobility and opportunity in an increasingly more challenging economic environment. Schools are expected to create purpose, order, motivation and a desire to learn when this is the student's responsibility.

On television: It is dependency on the talking heads to entertain, enlighten, shock, embarrass and excite in order to fill the menacing silence with distracting noise, to divert the mind from its function and unique singularity.

In the community: The syndrome is dependency on Law Enforcement and the Criminal Justice System to orchestrate morality, to be the community's conscience when the community has abdicated that responsibility. A community gets the police and justice system it deserves. If the community is hypocritical, violent or corrupt, the police will mirror that aspect.

A vast majority of workers find themselves in a "catch 22." They feel helpless and isolated on the one hand, and slaves to the system, captives to a world they did not create, on the other. They feel little obligation to challenge the system's integrity. They declare, "Not my problem!"

Workers sense the disorder in their lives, so they read, they listen to pundits on television, they surf the Internet, they explore apps on their iPads, they text and tweet, they look everywhere but to themselves for order. They argue among themselves. In the end they do what "the experts" say. Nothing changes, because they look always for change elsewhere, not in themselves. It has been my experience that most workers expect:

Management to be more responsive to workers' needs than workers are to the needs of the company that employs them.

Social services to be more accessible to workers' needs than workers are to the social needs of others.

Teachers and administrators to be more motivated to teach than students are motivated to learn.

Police to be more patient, tolerant and understanding of citizens and their needs, than citizens are willing to be respectful of police and understanding of the limits placed on police in the discharge of their duties.

Notice where the emphasis is placed? Always on others! It is always "somebody else's problem," not the workers'. You would think these service providers would challenge this absurdity. But rather than challenge these demands, these providers attempt to do the impossible.

Workers tend to identify their frustrations with causes outside themselves. These causes are packaged and promoted by self-interested experts, who have a stake in exploiting workers' self-indulgence. As long as workers are immature, on edge and self-ignorant, these promoters have a customer.

But it is all for naught. Outward order begins with inward order. There is no other way. A community, a company, a family gets better one person at a time. This is true in the case of economic parity, or matters of recognition, identity and social consciousness. It is equally true of government, science and religion. Government cannot do for the citizen what the citizen best do for himself. Nor can science forgive the A.I.D.'s epidemic by promising a miraculous cure for a social tic. Nor can religion celebrate the nobility of man by denying man's nature.

It is not the lack of leadership, alone, which is at fault. It is also the failure of workers to pay attention. Their lack of vigilance finds madness has gravitated to the collective norm. It is sanity that has become suspect. How do I prove this? I ask, "What has been your experience?"

Life is without cause. There is no direction, no safe harbor in sight. It puts me in mind of "The Flying Dutchman," the man on the legendary ship who can never make port, and is doomed to sail the ocean forever. Likewise, humanity never seems to find purchase of common ground on this planet. In microcosm, this is exercised in the 21st century by workers. They fail to see their self-interests and the collective self-interests of society as indistinguishable from each other. Everything starts and ends with the solitary worker, for each worker comes in alone and leaves alone. He comes out of nature and goes back into nature.

Man is still unfinished. He is only a recent inhabitant of earth, here no more than a few hundred thousand years. The purpose of his life is to live it, period. What he does is an expression of that purpose.

The problem with many workers is that they seem unable to see what is true from what is false. They want to be told. They wait. The wait freezes them in suspended adolescence, grown children who refuse to become adults, and fall back on being parents. How long will this be so? It is difficult to say. The prospects are not encouraging.

THE ASCENDENCY OF THE FEMININE PARADIGM

"Men have sight; women insight."
—**Victor Hugo** (1802-1885), French novelist and poet

Like all sciences and all valuations, the psychology of women has hitherto been considered only from the point of view of men . . . The question then is how far analytical psychology also, when in its researches have women for their object, is under the spell of this way of thinking, insofar as it has not yet wholly left behind the stage in which frankly and as a matter of course masculine development only was considered. In other words, how far has the evolution of women, as depicted to us today by analysis, been measured by masculine standards and how far therefore does this picture fail to present quite accurately the real nature of women.

—**Karen Horney,** *Feminine Psychology* (1967), pp. 56, 57.

NOBEL LAUREATE Paul Krugman suggests the march of technology leaves many behind.[1] University student Claire McNeill, a member of this technological digital generation sees no problem as "we will adapt and push on."[2] Joel Stein, Time magazine's columnist exuding in hyperboles sees Ms. McNeill's generation "the new greatest generation" and refers to it with the sobriquet, "the millennials."[3]

We have gone through a period of self-consciousness for the past forty years why should it be any surprise for the rise in ambivalence and optimism at once? We members of *The Great Depression* generation didn't have the luxury of ambivalence much less optimism. We had to act or get crushed by circumstances. Nor could we afford to take ourselves too seriously. Full attention of necessity was a matter of survival.

As we have moved from analog to digital, the hard and soft wiring of our brains has experienced a similar transport. By a curious predilection, we think in 3-D but reason in 2-D with linear logic and critical thinking. We venture into the world of the Internet but still fail to venture beyond what we know. What we don't know but can be found out takes creative thinking. We sometimes talk in hyperboles about the greatest this or that, but solve problems as if limited to an abacus.

Krugman relates that in the late 18th century the most skilled workers in the cloth industry were suddenly atavistic due to technology advancements. He makes passing reference to comfort being a factor in worker surprise. Comfort is the devil in the details.[4] The *Culture of Comfort* is potentially as debilitating to our world, as it was to those 18th century workers.

Given our linear orientation, the solution to modernity became better educated workers. So, everyone had to be a college graduate. This was the hysterical reaction in 1958 when the Soviet Union beat the USA into space with Sputnik. Not only did this fail to be the answer, but 57 years later, the skills learned by these highly trained people are proving too often anachronistic, as many recent college graduates can attest, or as Ms. McNeill says, cannot find work other than as "tempts," or in unpaid internships. More disturbing still, when Sputnik was launched, the United States was a global leader in education; in 2014, the US ranked seventeenth. Over the span of the last half-century, radical changes have been made in education, billions of dollars spent to regain this leadership, and yet it has proven mainly a vanilla response to the problem. Something is wrong with this formula.

Krugman confesses "education is no longer the answer. "What does he propose? A social safety net for all citizens. He is critical of capitalism, and there is a lot in capitalism that is worthy of criticism, but history has never been kind to society's that were asked to do more for their people than their people were asked to do for society.[5]

Paul Krugman, I'm sure, considers himself a rational economist if not a scientist, yet there is a decided *Utopian* aspect to his thinking. In one sense, it is reassuring given the dystopia of Aldous Huxley's *"Brave New World"* (1939) and George Orwell's *Nineteen Eighty-Four* (1949), which was inspired by Yevgeny Zamyatin's *We* (1924), a book set in the 26th century A.D. in the regimented totalitarian society of OneState ruled over by the all-powerful "Benefactor." These dystopian novels have proven startlingly prophetic. Krugman seems to have more in common with Edward Bellamy's American utopian novel, *Looking Backward* (1888). The year is 2000 for Bellamy's novel from his 1887 perspective, when the novel was written. Bellamy foresaw, as does Krugman, a managed society build on a social system based on justice, reason and solidarity. Alas, if only humans behaved as this novel depicts where there is no poverty, no war, little crime, and those in charge are engagingly unselfish and magnanimous.

Besides comfort and an inability to think other than critically on issues, Joel Klein mentions two others mindsets: optimism and narcissism. He presents some staggering insights:

- Millennials aren't trying to take over the establishment; they're growing up without one.
- The accelerating rates of narcissism, materialism and

technology are equally engaging to poor kids from the ghetto as to rich kids in the suburbs.

- Optimism is so rife that nearly half of all young people feel they should be promoted in their jobs regardless of their performance.
- The narcissistic personality is three times higher in people now in their 20s as people 65 and older.
- Most young people whatever their socioeconomic circumstances need a calculator to do simple math.
- The wave of the past few years to increase self-esteem has accidentally increased narcissism.

Christopher Lasch in *"The Culture of Narcissism"* (1978) foresaw 37 years ago that while young people would cling to optimism their unmet expectations would continue to rise. He writes:

"Today Americans are overcome not by the sense of endless possibility but by the banality of the social order they have erected against it. Having internalized the social restraints by means of which they formerly sought to keep possibility within civilized limits, they feel themselves overwhelmed by an annihilating boredom, like animals whose instincts have withered in captivitiy."[6]

Generational anxiety and angst is not new. Somehow, up to this point, we have survived the optimism, pathos and palliatives of each:

- Missionary Generation (1860-1882)
- The Lost Generation (1883-1900)
- The Greatest Generation (1901-1924)
- The Silent Generation-The Beat Generation (1925-1942)
- The Baby Boomer Generation (1943-1960)
- Generation X-Y and the Me-Generation (1961-1980)

- The Millennials (1980-2000)

Erik Erikson, German born developmental psychologist claims there are eight ages of man in his quest for maturity':

- Trust versus mistrust
- Autonomy versus doubt
- Initiative versus guilt
- Industry versus inferiority
- Identity versus role confusion
- Intimacy versus isolation
- Generativity versus stagnation
- Ego Integrity versus despair

High school teacher David McCullough, Jr. is pretty clear where he sees millennials in this continuum. In addressing Wellesley High School's graduating class, he reminded them, "You are not special. Climb the mountain so you can see the world not so the world can see you."

KEY ENCOUNTERS TO FEMININE LEADERSHIP

Each generation is reasonable or unreasonable, rational or irrational, moral, immoral or amoral largely on the basis of the predominant cognitive moral maturity in terms of how people think (reason) and interact (behave) with each other.

Women, in my experience, have had their feet firmly planted on the ground, pragmatically making the most of what little they sometimes have had, while their men would soar like birds carried away by their fantasies. Men essentially have created the world as we know it, a world of angst and anxiety, false hope and debilitating disappointment. It is time for women to bring men down to earth and back into reality by stepping out of the background and taking center stage.

The moral capacity of the problem solving is a reflection of learned behavior at earlier stages. Over the past 100 plus years there has been a demonstrable trend and tectonic shift that might be described as the *Feminine Paradigm*. This is not to be confused with the *Feminine Movement*, but a logical progression from transactional to transformational leadership essentially spirited by women. As women have come into their own it has impacted life, work and the way we think and behave.

Before we move on, it would be well to look briefly at the *feminine mystique* as perceived by the German psychiatrist and psychoanalyst Karen Horney (1885-1952).

She is a true pioneer in feminine psychology in questioning the relevance, in fact, the masculine Freudian dominance in the literature of psychology.

This was particularly true of her theories of sexuality and of the instinct orientation of psychoanalysis. She is credited with founding *Feminine Psychology* in response to Freud's Theory of *Penis Envy* and the *Castration Complex in Women*.

She disagreed with Freud about inherent differences in the psychology of men and women, and traced such differences to society and culture rather than biology. As such, she is often classified as *Neo-Freudian*.

Dr. Horney was also a pioneer in the discipline of feminine psychiatry. As one of the first female psychiatrists, she was the first of her gender to present a paper regarding feminine psychiatry.

The fourteen papers she wrote between 1922 and 1937 were amalgamated into a single volume titled *Feminine Psychology* (1967) published posthumously. Some of these papers are mentioned here.

As a woman, she felt that the mapping out of trends in female behavior was a neglected issue.

In her essay entitled *"The Problem of Feminine Masochism,"* Horney felt she proved that cultures and societies worldwide encouraged women to be dependent on men for their love, prestige, wealth, care and protection.

She pointed out that in society, a will to please, satisfy and overvalue men had emerged. Women were regarded as objects of charm and beauty—at variance with every human being's ultimate purpose of self-actualization.

Women, according to Horney, traditionally gain value only through their children and the wider family. She touched further on this subject in her essay *"The Distrust Between the Sexes"* in which she compared the husband-wife relationship to a parent-child relationship—one of misunderstanding and one which breeds detrimental neuroses.

Most notably her work *"The Problem of the Monogamous Ideal"* was fixed upon marriage, as were six other of her papers (all in *Feminine Psychology*).

Her essay *"Maternal Conflicts"* attempted to shed new light on the problems women experience when raising adolescents.

Dr. Horney believed that both men and women have a drive to be effective and productive. Women are able to satisfy this need normally and interiorly—to do this they become pregnant and give birth. Men please this need only through external ways. Horney proposed that the striking accomplishments of men in work or some other field can be viewed as compensation for their inability to give birth to children.

Dr. Horney also addressed her message to a popular audience releasing one of the first *"self-help"* books in 1946, entitled *"Are You Considering Psychoanalysis?"* (1962).

The book asserted that both men and women with relatively minor neurotic problems could, in effect, be their own psychiatrists. She continually stressed that self-awareness was a part of becoming a better, stronger, richer human being.

TRANSACTIONAL LEADERSHIP

Transactional leadership is a set of actions to attain explicit goals. The focus is on efficiency and follows the dictates of Frederick Winslow Taylor's *"Principles of Scientific Management"* (1911), where workers are things to be managed rather than persons to be led.[10] Efficiency is based on established policies, procedures and routines that are consistent with company directives leaving little wiggle room for change in the structure of doing business.

Later Management by Objectives (MBOs) was inserted to increase organizational efficiency as the corporation became a multiplex of many tiers of distinct functions and disciplines. At the same time, the Performance Appraisal System (PAS) was introduced in which supervisors judged worker traits (e.g., dependability, empathy, initiative, industry, fortitude, and ambition) as well as performance criteria on the job. PAS was meant to assess performance but became more of a device to solidify supervisory (management) control of workers with the objective of increased operating efficiency and productivity. It worked as long as workers behaved as "lethargically as oxen," as Taylor was wont to describe them.

Transactional leadership was managerial leadership. This emphasized the role of the supervisor to set group and individual standards. To improve managerial efficiency the concept of "leadership style" was adopted. Enter Douglas McGregor, Frederick Herzberg, Robert Blake and Jane Mouton, Rensis Likert, Paul Hershey and Ken Blanchard, and Abraham Maslow among a cadre of others."

Leadership styles promoted compliance not cooperation, which is coercive or externally generated through rewards and punishment. Cooperation is voluntary and internally generated through work itself and creative involvement.[12]

Sociological theories such as Peter Blau's *"Exchange and Power in Social Life"* (1964) and Abraham Maslow's Hierarchy of Needs in *'Motivation and Personality"* (1970) have risen out of transactional leadership. For example, *exchange and power relates to a quid pro quo* relationship between workers and managers where workers receive incentives and rewards for good work. Maslow developed a *"needs assessment"* tool to calibrate workers' needs from security to self-actualization.

Transactional leaders are concerned with processes not forward thinking ideas. Psychologist B.F. Skinner's behavioral modification theory applies where stimulus/response/reinforcement works much like Pavlov's dog, that is, contingent rewards (incentives/praise) and punishment (disincentives/criticism) lead to mechanical and passive responsive behavior and management by exception. Problems aren't anticipated; they are reacted to once they occur.

This promotes passive leadership, which confines the problem solving to thinking "inside the box" with linear logic, cause and effect analysis, *a priori* reasoning, and critical thinking with little ambition to think beyond what is known and has worked somewhere before.

Transactional Leadership, in summary:

- Leadership is responsive to perturbations rather than anticipating them.
- Works within the traditional organizational culture.
- Objectives are realized through rewards and punishment.
- Motivation follows the leadership's self-interest and biases.
- Management by exception maintains the status quo.
- Management exercises infallible authority.
- Business as usual practices persist no matter the disruptive crisis.
- Control is indisputably in the hands of management.

TRANSFORMATIONAL LEADERSHIP

Historian James MacGregor Burns has been a student of leadership most of his life bringing the idea of transactional-transformational leadership to the fore with his book *"Leadership"* (1978) and subsequently, *"Transforming Leadership: A New Pursuit of Happiness"* (2003).

Traits are emphasized in transactional leadership while the situation is dominant in transformational leadership. Likewise, in transactional leadership survival (security) needs at the lower end in the *Maslow's Hierarchy of Needs* are emphasized whereas self-actualizing needs at the apex are emphasized in transformational leadership.

Transformational leadership differs in several other ways from transactional leadership:

- Followers are emphasized instead of leaders
- Enabling rather than directing
- Aims towards values — life, liberty, justice, opportunity, and empowerment in pursuit of happiness
- Is proactive rather than responsive
- Works to change to change the organizational culture rather than defend the status quo organization

- Motivates to put group interests above personal
- Is intellectually challenging and stimulating
- Has a different approach to power
- Appeals to the moral side of doing business
- Focuses on beliefs, needs and values of followers
- Leaders and followers are partners in synergizing activities to raise one another to higher levels of motivation and morality
- Cares about the individual and the team
- Stimulates a sense of ownership and meaning in work
- Raises the level of moral conduct and ethical aspirations
- Creates a dynamic versus the static environment of transactional leadership
- Leaders are often introverted and reserved not given to eloquent speeches or charismatic magnetism
- Leaders have a deep sense of purpose as do their followers

Most leaders display a combination of both transactional and transformational leadership, but for the past 60-70 years the dominant form in most cases has been the former. For example, transactional moral value leadership is process or means oriented:

- Honesty
- Responsibility
- Fairness
- Honoring one's commitments

Transformational moral value leadership is transcendent or ends oriented. Transcendent values include:

- Liberty
- Justice
- Equality
- Collective well being

One of the criticisms of James MacGregor Burns is his reliance on Erik Erikson's psychoanalytical typology of the family." Transformational leadership is also decidedly intellectual as it is devoted to ideas and values that transcend immediate practical needs with an interest in changing the culture to provide a fertile climate for future challenges.

Psychoanalyst Karen Horney, looking at leadership from a feminine rather than a masculine perspective, emphasizes self-understanding and self-awareness which emanates from an authentic self, what I have referred to in my writing as *possessing a moral compass with a moral center guidance system.*

To lead others, Horney insists, the leader must first have control of him or herself, which means leadership development evolves from self-development. This makes self-understanding and self-awareness crucial to the process.

It amounts to conscious competence in pursuit of the *Culture of Contribution,* whereas transactional leadership often gets bogged down in unconscious incompetence *(Culture of Comfort)* or conscious incompetence *(Culture of Complacency)* while using excessive incentives to spark productive efforts. [14]

Scholars contend there is no gender bias but that has not been my experience. It has led to this focus on the *Feminine Style of Leadership,* which is caring, and nurturing and more transformational than transactional in its ascendancy. To state this simply:

- The focus of attention is on behavior and action.
- It is goal-directed activity but of a difference.
- It models positive behavior where leaders and followers are on the same page and getting off on the same dime.
- The emphasis is on empowerment and initiative without having to make this a program.

As organizational power and decision-making is increasingly decentralized, as worker become more pliable and open, as identity politics and role relationships continue to blur, the feminine connection promises to quietly rise to the forefront.

Dr. Horney shows how the *idealized self* under the influence of the *Super Ego* (the *Parent* in transactional terms) derails leadership. The focus is on "should dos" as self-demands dominate.

This is at the expense of role demands (i.e., the requirements of the work at hand) or the *real self* (the *Adult* in transactional terms).

See the "Fisher Model of Conflict and Stress Resolution" *(Six Silent Killers: Management's Greatest Challenge).*

THE ASCENDENCY INTO THE NEW FEMININE PARADIGM

This ascendency has been broader than leadership although it includes leadership. It has been phasic consistent with the shift in American values from the common good and tradition to personhood and individualism, as noted in *"Work Without Managers"* (1991):

- Authority has shifted from position power to knowl-

edge power.
- Loyalty has shifted from loyalty to the organization to oneself and one's peers or profession.

- Discipline has shifted from rewards and/or punishment to caring and respect, even love.
- Motivation has shifted from fear or external pressure outside oneself to challenge and contribution or self-satisfaction and pride within oneself.

In *Work Without Managers (1991),* I write:

"This difference has already had pivotal ramifications across America, from the home to the workplace. Adversaries have been made of parents and children, teachers and students, the clergy and laity, managers and workers, leaders and followers. This shift in values has produced a perceptible gap between expectations and achievements in the complex organization.

"So traumatic has the situation become that many parents, educators, executives, clergy and leaders are abandoning the conflict. They have abdicated their responsible roles in frustration, proclaiming that they are powerless'."[15]

Later, in *"Corporate Sin: Leaderless Leaders & Dissonant Workers"* (2000), an attempt is made to show managers and professionals in collusion in this tailspin into incompetence (see *"The Quiet Transition to the Feminine Paradigm of Organization"*).[16]

Suggested here is that the feminine style of leadership is superseding the masculine style of leadership which has dominated the human group since time immemorial.

The expectations of men are active and productive compared to passive and receptive for women. Men are rational and cognitive while women are insightful and intuitive. Men are aggressive, competitive and ruthless; women are responsive, cooperative and consolidating. Men are conscious of themselves as thinkers;

women are conscious of their environment as feelers. Men are inclined towards quantitative thinking and science; women are inclined toward qualitative thinking and abstraction.

"Meanwhile, power has shifted from the exclusive domain of the management elite to the sharing of power with professional workers. What was once considered work, meeting the demands and expectations of management, has all but disappeared. Management still goes through the motions and acts as if nothing has changed, but it no longer has exclusive power or control. Management stubbornly resists reality, which contributes to the dissonance of workers."[17]

In explaining the *Feminine Paradigm* in *Corporate Sin*, I ask the reader to consider where he sees men and women in this typology:

- Knower vs. learner.
- Teller vs. listener.
- "We have the answer" vs. "People have the answer."
- Data driven vs. conceptual clarification of information.
- Competitive winning vs. cooperative sharing.
- "Value free" critical thinking vs. "value added" creative thinking.
- Quantitative analysis vs. qualitative assessment.
- Circular liner logic vs. intuitive insight.
- Aggressive engagement vs. consensus alliance.
- Comfort vs. contribution. [18]

This quiet transition can be seen in the corporate movement from the dominance of vertical thinking (linear logic, quantitative analysis) to the complement of lateral thinking (conceptual discernment), from the arrogance of the *Masculine Paradigm* to the unassuming nature of the *Feminine Paradigm*. With the latter paradigm, no one succeeds unless everyone does."

The digital *Information Age* with its ever expanding Internet has changed many things not the least of which is the hard wiring of our brains. We all have left and right lobes to our brains but popular culture has designated the left brain "masculine" and the right brain "feminine." Here are some contrasting functions of this bicameral mind:

Left Brain	Right Brain
Demanding	Contracting
Aggressive	Responsive
Competitive	Cooperative
Rational/Cognitive/Analytical	Intuitive/Affective/Synthesizing
Concrete Orientation	Conceptual Orientation

Proof that we have hit the wall with the infallibility of traditional authority and doing business as usual no matter how many times it proves disastrous is apparent with Wall Street and the automotive industry in the wake of the financial collapse of 2008. Moreover, study organizational charts of 1950 and compare them to 2015 and you can see why the schizophrenic organization persists. Neither the transactional or transformational leadership has dealt with this problem. It is necessary to go beyond for these reasons:

- Workers' values have changed.
- Relationships between workers and managers have changed.
- The critical mass of work has changed from brawn to brains, from activity to information, from doing to thinking, from producing to serving, from concrete indices to symbolic interaction.
- The *Information Age* does not reside in management.
- What constitutes work has shifted from working hard to working smart.[20]
- We are truly on the threshold of a new day.

ARRIVAL OF MILLENNIALS

The current generation known as the "millennials" are not trying to take over the establishment, nor to fall in line with its hierarchical authority. Instead, they are choosing to ignore the establishment and grow up without it.

They are accused of being lazy, narcissistic, not centered, going with the flow, and even being unhinged. While being indifferent to such criticism, they look past the establishment's hyperbole, rhetoric, chicanery, duplicity, backstabbing, and climate of chasing shadows in society's nervous dance to paranoia.

Millennials, reared in a climate of reality television, are living their lives as if defined by reality television at the age of fourteen, while their parents are still struggling with identity at the age of forty.

While their parents had a problem with authority, with its infallible finality, millennials don't pay it much mind. They are the first generation not interested in rebelling against the status quo, mainly because it has never been a threat to their take on life. Moreover, they seem to know in their bones the problems they face can't be solved within the status quo, because they are problems of the status quo. Nor are millennials given to the herd mentality of "true believers" bent on a mission to establish a counterculture. It would be hard for them to join such a culture when, from their perspective, there is no culture. They see themselves starting out from scratch.

They are creatures of smartphones, laptops, apps and the Internet, which they see has democratized them and given them access to information that once only belonged to the powerful and wealthy. A lot of what counts as millennial behavior is how rich kids have always behaved. Millennials, however, at opposite ends of the food chain are behaving pretty much the same, which calls for some study.

Consequently, they are not intimidated by position or knowledge power, and therefore can negotiate much better contracts for themselves with traditional institutions.

This generation thinks before it does, and is usually thinking three or four steps ahead of its interlocutors. They tell recruiters, "I want to do this, and then when that is done, I want to do this."

It is too late for the traditional organization to wield its power in this confusion because they are here and they are earnest and optimistic, pragmatic and idealists, tinkerers more than dreamers, life hackers rather than trendsetters, gender and ethnic neutral seeing the world flat with the mantra, "May the best person win whoever that might be."

It is yet to be established if they can lead or follow as they cannot escape some of the hash tags that obsessed their parents such as the need for constant approval.

Check out their posted photos on the social Internet. They also fear missing out, cannot stand silence, or being alone, and have to always be doing something. They are celebrity obsessed and have an acronym for everything. They don't go to church but believe in God and are likely to be religiously unaffiliated.

In case this is worrisome, they are cool, reserved, not all that passionate, and therefore less prone to manipulation. They are also pro-business, financially responsible although student loans are more than a $trillion, but household and credit card debt is less than any previous generation.

In terms of numbers, they are the largest generation in United States history. Ergo, no recitation of "empowerment" need be voiced as they see themselves as empowered, in charge, comfortable before a camera and able to articulate their case.

Millennials embrace the future by living in the present, and what they make of it promises to be very different than what they have inherited from their parents and society.

They are not handicapped by the litany of go to school and get good grades, as they see the absurdity of the elevated grading system, resulting in social promotion. They know colleges and universities depend on defense and industrial contracts for survival, while pretending they do not. This hypocrisy was bothersome to their parents, but not to them.

Nor are millennials troubled with what they have been told is true only to find it is not, such as living in an open, free society of equal opportunity when they see that is not true of people of color, or of women compared to men of their parents' generation. They plan on making it true, however, for theirs.

They have been inundated with cultural values that don't resonate. Self-esteem is claimed to be essential when they see it is great in getting a job or hooking up with someone at a bar, but not so great keeping a job or a relationship. They are left with the idea that has become close to a cause, which is to distance themselves from anything and everything that suggests "the establishment."[21]

Resources

1. Paul Krugman, "March of technology leaves many behind," Tampa Bay Times, 6/17/13, p. 9A.
2. Claire McNeill, "My digital generation adapts and pushes on, "Tampa Bay Time, 6/14/13, p. 15A
3. Joel Stein, "The New Greatest Generation: Why Millennial Will Save Us All," Time magazine, 5/20/13, pp. 27-34.
4. Kurgan, op. cit.
5. This is a variation of John F. Kennedy's Inaugural Address as he assumed the presidency in 1961. What is not common knowledge is that the poet Kahlil Gibran uttered it to the people of Lebanon in 1925: *`Are you a politician asking what your country can do for you or a zealous one asking what you can do for your country?"*
6. Christopher Lash: *"The Culture of Narcissism: American Life in An Age of Diminishing Expectations,"* W.W. Norton & Company, 1978, p. 11.
7. Erik H. Erikson, *"Childhood and Society,"* W.W. Norton & Company, 1963, pp. 247-274.
8. Stein, Op. Cit., pp. 27-32.
9. James R. Fisher, Jr., *"Corporate Sin: Leaderless Leaders & Dissonant Workers,"* AuthorHouse 2000, pp. 177-201.
10. Frederick Winslow Taylor, *"The Principles of Scientific Management,"* W.W. Norton & Company, 1967, p. 59.
11. Douglas McGregor, *"The Human Side of Enterprise,"* 1960; Frederick Hertzberg, *"Work and the Nature of Man,"* 1966; Robert Black and Jane Mouton, *"The Managerial Grid,"*

1964; Rensis Likert, *"The Human Group: Its Management and Values,"* 1967; Paul Hershey and Kenneth Blanchard, *"The Human Group: Its Management and Values,"* 1972; Abraham Maslow, *'Motivation and Personality,"* 1970.
12. James R. Fisher, Jr., *"Six Silent Killers: Management's Greatest Challenge,"* CRC Press, 1998, pp. 120-121.
13. Erik Erikson, *"Identity, Youth and Crisis,"* W.W. Norton and Company, 1968, pp. 115-121.
14. Fisher, Op. Cit., 143-220.
15. *Work Without Managers: A View from the Trenches,* AuthorHouse, Bloomington, IN, 1991, pp. 33-34.
16. *Corporate Sin,* pp. 177-121.
17. Ibid, 179-180.
18. Ibid, 188-190.
19. David M. Boje, *"Transformational Leadership,"* Internet, 12/25/00, pp. 1-37.
20. Op. Cit., *Corporate Sin,* p. 186.
21. Op. Cit., Joel Stein, pp. 27-32.

THE MASCULINE PARADIGM

MARRIED TO THE MACHINE!

ARCHITECTS OF A FAILED SYSTEM!

"The path to joy leads through despair."
—**Alexander Lowen,** physician and psychotherapist

IT IS TIME we admit that efforts to correct the cultural slide of society as it relates to workers has failed. It is time we get inside these failures and examine them for what they are. By doing so, most problems can be solved. Three crucial flaws contribute to the social psychological chaos of our times:

Workers have failed to seize the moment as mature adults. Mature adults are workers who accept reality instead of being obsessed with "what should be," or "has been," or "what's going to be." What we have, in the main, are workers as dependent children in a world which stubbornly refuses to grow up. These workers have the disposition, inclination, collective identity and impulsive rashness of children. They don't want the facts, they want more, and they want it now! They fail to realize feelings are facts, and nothing changes until they change themselves.

Workers are predominantly knowers, not learners. Our entire educational system produces knowers, not learners; apologists, not thinkers. Most workers learn a skill, a craft or profession, and then coast for forty years, essentially inattentive to what is happening around them, and then call it a career. This necessitates the invention of media pundits, pseudo-specialists, armchair scholars, and high priests of science and religion to fill the void. These omniscient promulgators dictate to workers what to think, feel, value, believe and expect. Lost here is that "experts" wallow in the same confusion as workers. Few are learners, only knowers.

Workers are obsessed with control. Control is everything. Few realize the absurdity of this obsession. Yet, the evidence is emphatic. The more workers attempt to control their nature the more nature controls them. It is equally so in the general as in the particular. Man delights in the conquest of nature, and has for centuries, treating nature as if a separate entity. And so the planet is out-of-control. The controller and the controlled are but one and the same. Everything is related to the same whole. Unfortunately, a wedge has been driven between the mind and the body; between earth and man. Division is celebrated, not communion.

Viewed in the particular, the more workers attempt to control their passions, appetites and behaviors, the less they control them. Good intentions count for little. Deeds, not words, make the difference. How could it be otherwise?

Control is a maddening societal pursuit, which fractures, segments and isolates. An obsession with control creates chaos, not order. But *Mechanistic Man* cannot think otherwise. A mechanistic mentality thinks in terms of separation, not connection; of conflict, not harmony; of the parts, not the whole. *Mechanistic Man* would find it strange for one to propose that he think with his whole body.

Yet virtually everything is connected; everything is related—subject to object; object to subject; cause to effect; effect to cause. Resolving a problem in the context of the part always creates another problem, often worse than the problem resolved.

Resolution can only be realized when control is suspended and order is embraced. But order requires "letting go," which is practically unfathomable for a mechanistic mind.

The essence is that the root to maturity necessitates embracing our fears, and not retreating from them, recognizing that engagement and success involve struggle, disappointment and failure, that problems are never solved but only controlled, that this necessitates adaptation, as nothing is fixed but constantly changing, which calls for cooperation and commitment from us all, as we thrive or perish together.

Subsequently, we will discuss these flaws in more detail. For now, consider the impact of these fixations on behavior. Obviously, these flaws derail a good number of workers from satisfying lives. What workers' think, they become. If the work they do is mainly thought to be bogus, then it follows their lives can hardly be considered genuine. Consider this:

> *A gainfully employed worker, firmly ensconced in reality, is more likely to develop and use his skills in the service of others, and therefore experience happiness. Happiness is not the absence of sorrow, but inseparable from joy. Pleasure is also married to pain; success to failure; certainty to doubt; clarity to confusion, and so on. Happiness has peaks and valleys, for good and bad days are part of the same experience. With this perspective, a happy worker is unlikely to harm his coworker or commit suicide; is not likely to become a criminal or a child molester. A happy worker is humble in the sight of his Creator and a law abider; not one to covet either another's property or person. A happy worker is the foundation of a rational ordering society.*

Now that we have established this premise, the question must be asked, whose responsibility is it for the worker to be happy? The workers of course. The crux of society's problem is that this is not clearly understood or accepted. Happiness is about being, about living moment to moment as best a person can. Happiness is not about becoming, or achieving, not about comparing, or competing, not about security, and certainly, not about control. Happiness is a state of mind. Once you try to analyze it, you lose it. Happiness is experienced in psychological time, not chronological time.

Psychological time is in the moment, whereas chronological time is of the past or the future, finding little comfort in the present. Psychological time is about love, love of life, love of self, love of others, love of work, of comfort with what is. Psychological time is about giving, chronological time is about getting, psychological time is about what needs to be done, chronological time is about what can be avoided, psychological time is about being, chronological time is about becoming. Therefore, psychological time is adaptable to circumstances. Is it any wonder that our obsession with chronological time has made us unhappy and discontented?

NOT HAPPY CAMPERS!

"Happiness is something to experience, not explain. Once you attempt to explain it, you lose it."

—**Alan W. Watts,** British born philosopher

IT WOULD APPEAR most workers are not happy campers and live in quiet desperation. It matters little whether these workers are surviving on unemployment compensation, or managing six figure incomes. The melancholy is similar. Sixty percent of high achievers, according to one study, felt they had sacrificed far too much in pursuit of material rewards. They sensed they had sacrificed their identity and wasted years of their lives, and for what? These successful workers, many senior level executives, admitted to putting on a front of being cool,rational thinkers, while three out of four confessed to depending mainly on feelings and intuitions for their decisions. Moreover, outwardly they appeared impervious to criticism and disapproval, whereas three out of five admitted to craving acceptance, recognition and approval. These workers, at opposite ends of the food chain, are tense, depressed, preoccupied and consumed with fear, as if the burden of the world were on their shoulders. Senior level executives, unemployed or underemployed workers share several disturbing attributes in common. They are surprisingly dull witted, humorless, culturally impoverished, shamelessly self-indulgent and as interesting to talk to as hearing the want ads read aloud. They don't stretch their minds, but on rare occasion exercise their hamstrings. Conditioned to react, not act; to complain, not communicate, they are consummate spectators to life, while pretending to be "hard chargers" and to have "no time." Secretly, they want to be entertained, not challenged; to vegetate, not think. Such lethargy spawns a cadre of celebrities to fill their empty heads.

These workers work for money, not self-realization or self-fulfillment. It would be career limiting for anyone to come out of the closet and declare himself a *bona fide* intellectual, or God forbid!—an elitist!

Democracy loves mediocrity, but abhors, in equal measure, brilliance, idiosyncrasy, genius, or curmudgeons of any kind. Film action heroes, professional athletes and celebrity murderers compete for this worker's limited attention span. The media give these "superstars" more exposure in twenty four hours than an iconoclastic Richard Feynman or a cerebral Isaiah Berlin receives in a lifetime.

It has been my experience that:

College professors read little more than the general public. Check their class notes. Most are ancient. If class notes are less than ten years old, you're dealing with a neophyte. Tenure is a communicable disease supportive of academic indolence.

Medical doctors don't pursue their professions much beyond

what is required. Quiz your personal physician sometime for confirmation. They coast with the same rhythm as the lathe operator.

Psychiatrists talk in meaningless psychobabble. The fact is we have made little progress in predicting human behavior. Moreover, research has shown psychiatrists know little more about the workings of the human mind than the average citizen on the street. Psychiatrists are essentially psycho-pharmacologists.

Most engineers in this mechanistically driven society would re-engineer our social systems without a modicum of understanding of the human soul, which they refuse to accept exists.

For every problem the scientific community solves, two new problems surface in the social system. Should this alarm you, ask yourself: Is this world actually a better, safer, healthier and more pleasant place in which to live than it was 200 years ago?

Anyone who has had the sad experience of being embroiled in litigation knows they could better represent themselves than most attorneys. Yet, we have a plethora of this breed. In most major cities, there is one attorney for every 30-40 citizens; in Washington, D. C. this ratio balloons to one in twelve, yet this is considered not nearly enough according to the *Washington Examiner*. A statistic that is not commonly shared from legal scholars is that many towns and municipalities have more attorneys than they can afford to support, yet thousand more are graduated from our colleges and universities every year.

Between 600,000 and 1,000,000 new books are published each year. Yet, according to a Huffington Post Survey, 40 percent or 128 million Americans do not read a book a year. Most millennials don't read newspapers getting most of their information on-line.

Few Europeans, and even fewer Asians admit to reading American authors outside of technology. They claim most American fiction is intellectually uninspiring.

Ignoring these data, mass marketers continue to fill the glutted book publishing industry with e-books from such electronic producing outlets as Amazon.com. One day soon electronic books in the Cloud may exceed the U.S. National Debt, which is now in the $trillions.

Then there is the vanity press, which has been around since WWII but is now flourishing. It exploits the conceit that "everyone's an author," although such books usually fail to find an audience outside of family and friends. Vanity publishers get rich exploiting this "lotto like" cultural sickness. Meanwhile, 14 percent or some 44 million Americans have such poor or non-existing reading skills that they cannot read the words printed here. Go figure!

If the book publishing industry has us flummoxed, then what should we make of corporate vagaries?

The majority of corporate enterprises, and this extends to the academic and healthcare field as well, claim to promote the idea of a meritocracy. In actual practice, *courtiers extraordinaire* are likely to get the majority of the plum promotions.

Consequently, the main ingredient to "making it" appears to be corporate *connections*.

Therefore, it behooves the *pyramid climber,* who personifies the corporate sycophant, to be amenable to the CEO's pet projects no matter how insane or inane.

Yet, despite this charade, workers in the trenches are inclined to pay fawning homage to executive mediocrity without protest no matter how destabilizing to their situation. They echo the sentiments, "It is not our call!"

What they mean is that should the corporation go belly up they need a "fall guy," and it won't be *them!*

The whimpering "we" (workers) take solace in the blame game

that "they" (corporate decision-makers) did it to us and *"We had nothing to do with it (the outcome),"* which is unlikely to be the case.

Most workers within my experience see themselves as paid to do, not to think, create, change, or improve, not even to feedback to management systemic discrepancies. Most workers fail to see themselves as part of the problem, and therefore outside the solution. Whatever management's decision, appropriate or not, represents no risk to them, "No skin off our teeth."

There is no attempt here to minimize the problem between workers and managers. There are no simple remedies.

Take the automotive industry. Since 1982, the United Auto Workers (UAW), given the precarious position of the American automotive industry, has felt unable to bridge the growing gap that has materialized in the UAW's relationship with the "Big Three": General Motors, Ford and Chrysler.

Consequently, presidents of the UAW over the past thirty years have been obliged to make concessions consistent with the policy "that the contract must protect the corporation's competitiveness." In other words, the contract must be in the "interest of the corporation" irrespective of the National Labor Relations Board's stated guidelines that the role of labor is to negotiate "wages, working conditions and hours of work in the interest of the members."

This has been the policy over the past thirty years, but even with such concessions on the part of labor, General Motors and Chrysler as well as Wall Street in 2008 had to be "bailed out" by the federal government during that year's total economic collapse as they were deemed "too big to fail."

The UAW has in excess of 139,000 members who have written hundreds of pages of how to improve operations, reduce costs, and reestablish a partnership between labor and management, but to no avail.

As this was being written, GM was stepping up production of pickup trucks at its Wentzville, Missouri plant while trimming lunch breaks and hiring extra weekend staff to fill the surprisingly strong demand for midsize pickups and commercial vans.

Clearly, workers were not considered. They have dealt with this slight by posting scores of juvenile and petty outrages on social media.

This will have little or no impact on the problem, but illustrates the dilemma, or why the worker has no other option than going against the grain!

Anything which cuts to the core of the problem should be an embarrassment to everyone, not just management. Yet workers maneuver themselves to be outside embarrassment. They stand on the sidelines and scoff at management's ineptitude, feeling little sense of the implied irony. Workers, in the main, are fatalists, "Do with me what you will!" — paid robots, not thinkers or managers of what they do, and of course always beyond Harm's Way. This is a shared indictment of the lily fingered professionals as much as it is the grubby gloved blue collar workers.

Workers have adopted a passive posture for reason. When a worker thinks for himself, takes a stand, goes against the grain of the prevailing norms, or fails to go along with the silent majority, all hell is likely to break loose. If into sports, they might justify their inaction by saying, "Look at what happened to Curtis Flood in baseball, when he took a stand. "They would get a very different take, however, if they read Curtis Flood's biography *(Stepping Up* by Alex Belth and Tim McCarver, 2006).

First, the worker in question is labeled anything from trouble-maker, maverick, gadfly, exploiter, disrupter, provocateur, upstart to bad influence. Once the labeling is secured, and the meek join in the name bashing, the "upstart" is given a humiliating assignment, demotion, or is selectively ostracized from the group. No one wants to be caught dead talking to him.

In not too subtle ways, the worker who thinks for himself is subjected to a campaign of psychic duress. This may include not being invited to lunch with peers, not being copied on departmental memos, or notified of meeting changes, while being harassed with constant kidding and put downs. If not treated as an outsider, he is treated as if invisible. Ultimately, the tormentors get their wish. He quits or is let go.

On rare occasions, even this *persona non grata* treatment fails to move the "upstart." Should this be the case, he is the first casualty of downsizing. The majority observe this and adopt a subservient posture, the demeanor of "the victim." The best workers thereafter operate at about 40 percent efficiency, and frantically watch their backs. They never know when the other shoe will fall.

Cynicism is a function of lost hope. Cynics know little about workers. They actually consider workers different than managers, more or less as children. Obviously, managers are needed to control these children. Cynics believe workers have little sense of the common good, that they are dominated by self-interests; that their perspective is exclusively on short-term gains (raises), not long-term benefits (careers). Guess what? Workers don't disappoint. They behave as children, even as incorrigible children.

"Keep your nose clean! Don't get in the way of the boss!" This is the workers' code of survival. If the boss is incompetent and the operation goes to seed, "Well, that is the way the ball bounces!" When the plant closes, the buildings turn to eyesores, the town dries up, and there is no work anymore, who is to blame? Never the workers. Self-determined *learned helplessness* and ignorance absolves them of any collusion in their own self-tragedy.

Most workers within my experience take it on the chin as

victims far more often than they fight for their jobs and rights as victors. They behave as dependent children to management, or counter dependent adolescents to the company. Workers fail to fight for their jobs because behaving as children, they have never learned how to pay attention.

This could not happen to mature adults for reason:

Mature adult workers question work related decisions initiated by top management, because such direction is far removed from "where the rubber hits the road," and therefore is not necessarily an informed status of the work situation at hand. Mature adults put their special knowledge to work at the level of consequences in a timely fashion where problems occur. Mature adult workers find it easier to ask forgiveness than permission when something vital to operations must be done, now!

Mature adult workers question a company's aberrations, such as its obsession with productivity at any cost, while chronic problems not addressed in the system impact the profitability of that productivity. Mature adult workers question a company's philosophy that focuses on "not losing" rather than driving hard "to win."

Lagging production and failure to cultivate new markets ultimately translates into lost jobs and reduced security. If the market is shrinking, mature adult workers want a voice in why. Perhaps they have ideas which could make for a turnaround.

Mature adult workers question entitlement benefit packages. These are treated like Christmas candy, which implies undeserved generosity of the company, for they are infrequently tied to results. *Mature adult workers* know there is no free lunch. They have seen their real wages decline precipitously, and their benefit packages, too. They want an end to the charade. Mature adult workers want the company to level with them, to treat them as full partners in enterprise, not just hired help. Executives are employees, too.

Executives have no more stake in the company's future than they do — perhaps even less. Mature adult workers have a long term commitment to the company, while many executives attempt to put the best face on their watch in the interest of short-term career mobility.

Mature adult workers don't need to be told their worth. They know their worth. They don't need to be romanced with "touchy-feely" human resources programs. These manipulative ploys turn them off and tune them out. They want full accountancy of the company's health on a regular basis, not when the company is about to go belly up.

They resent the patronizing twaddle that attempts to keep them in line. They desire straight talk, a reasonable voice in the conduct of business and a fair portion of the economic pie.

Mature adult workers resent slogans, campaigns, fads and copycat programs. What worked elsewhere was unique to that operation. A plethora of failures in copy-cat programs, however, fails to push this fact home. Mature adult workers question the emphasis on "quality participation," when they see themselves herded into improvised meetings, where the level of discussion is restricted to nonoperational incidentals while executives, "down the hall," vote themselves stock options for the next quarter. Selective differentiation hardly begets teamwork or quality performance. Nor does the frenzied pursuit of quality awards mean much to mature adult workers. They see quality in explainable *statistical Six Sigma terms* as a daily concern and not as corporate gamesmanship.

Quality is not an exercise. Quality is a mindset. Mature adult workers focus on the "vital few" problems that make 80 percent of the difference in operations instead of on the "trivial many" problems that have only a 20 percent impact. The "vital few" problems require focusing on doing the "right things," whereas the "trivial many" problems has the focus of "doing everything right the first time."

With "quality participation," management has unwittingly created a menu of "the trivial many" problems with the mantra, "do everything right the first time," which is not only absurdly impossible but counterproductive.

If workers were 100 percent successful in this activity, since the "trivial many" make up only 20 percent of the difference in operations, 80 percent of the operational problems would remain untouched. Mature adult workers know this. Doing everything "right" sounds good as a campaign, or makes for an impressive executive presentation, but it sponsors cheating. Doing the "right things," on the other hand, encourages ingenuity, cooperation, teamwork and sponsors real achievement. Workers can get excited about this, for it moves the company off the dime, and gives them a sense of pride in their role. They know they have made a difference. They don't have to be told. Knowing spurs them on to even higher performance.

Mature adult workers question the value of rhetoric, which advocates a culture of contribution, but supports the twin cultures of comfort and complacency. A culture of contribution is dynamic, rife with conflict and confrontation, a spirited exchange of ideas of equal partners. Conflict, not harmony, is the glue that holds a company to its purpose. Mature adult workers recognize pain, risk, uncertainty, failure and limits as necessary components of real performance. An investment in failure is acknowledged as the price of success.

Mature adult workers question cosmetic organizational changes brought on by real or imagined crises. Mature adults abhor solution driven approaches to structural problems, which they see as, at best, naïve if not faddish appeasements to stockholders.

They recognize that defining the problem is hard work, and nigh impossible if the working culture is driven by personality, not performance; by making an impression, not a difference. Making an impression has no place in a climate of purposefulness. Where making a difference matters, there is no fear of failure, so success can take hold; no place for arrogance, so confidence can be expressed; no need for pretension, so happy debate can lead to consensus strategies.

Mature adult workers are threatening, not only to the company, but to the existing social fabric of society. From attending school to taking a job, from paying homage to the church to the state, from birth to death, citizens are expected to behave essentially as obedient, disciplined, punctual and not problem children. Schools teach students to conform to authority. Jobs are described and managed in the same manner. The tenets of religious faith are written as if to starry-eyed children, while the conduct of government could not demonstrate a lower opinion of the human species.

Society is afraid of mature adult workers, afraid of the madness that adulthood demands, for with such madness things are seen much more clearly than by those who claim to be sane. Ergo, they see society running from itself, cowering behind its authority and autocratic rule. The evidence is overwhelming. Self-hatred is manifested in society in the form of violence and crime. Love no longer recreates itself. Love has been replaced by pervasive hatred, which has become like the rich, aromatic stench of the garbage dump.

A paternalistic driven society prefers that workers never grow up, that they remain perpetually obedient, submissive, indulgent and manageable children. With mature adult workers, control no longer resides in the parent-figure as overlord. It is in the mind, heart and hands of workers, where it belongs. The agony of our times is that children become parents, but skip adulthood. Parent-figures, as an ideal-type, bully their children as they had been bullied. Bullying behavior is then repeated with family members, workers, worshippers, students and finally, with citizens. Failing to become mature adults, workers regress to learned helplessness and seek guidance, direction and control as if suspended in terminal adolescents as obedient twelve-year-olds in fifty-year-old bodies. Despite this characterization, the redemption of society still depends on the production of mature adult workers.

Even if the dedicated mission of society were to produce mature adult workers, it would most likely take the better part of a century to see it realized. Cultural conditioning of modern workers is that extensive. Most workers are programmed in self-negation, feeling a compelling need to conform to group norms, to avoid conflict and confrontation at any cost, to comply with arbitrary standards no matter how ridiculous, rather than to cooperate with a sense of commitment to something meaningful and to which they can believe.

Most workers value the thoughts of others over their own thoughts. They are isolated from a sense of their own worth. It would be as impossible for them to think differently as to defy gravity and fly.

It would appear they are not happy campers; that they have lost their moral compass and thus their way. In the end as in the beginning, what is invaluable to the individual, worker and citizen alike, is trust. No trust is more important than self-trust.

THE CHALLENGE OF LEARNING!

"We have designed organizations which ignored individual potential for competence, responsibility and constructive intent and productivity."
—Chris Argyris, American business theorist

LEARNING REQUIRES DISCIPLIN, but not conformity that most disciplines display. Conformity isolates workers. It places them in cages of fear. In the past half century this fear has manifested itself in a mad dash "to be educated" with little apparent interest in learning in the process. The acronyms BA, BS, MA, MS, PhD, MBA, DD, MD, BSEE, BSME, BSCE, and so on, do not connote learning or the ability to learn, but the accumulation of knowledge of the known.

Ironically, such labels can be acquired with practically no learning taking place. It does not necessarily follow that being "educated," you are educable. Education has become an industry with a factory mentality. It produces a product that doesn't always value learning. That said many graduates, once they run into that first career disappointment, return to university for yet another degree without sorting out why they have encountered this early impasse.

Learning comes from life, and life is all about experience. Emerson (1803-1882) in his essay *"Experience "speaks* out against the efforts to over-intellectualize life, which finds us departing from the real and drifting into the *ideal,* or now in the 21st century into the *surreal.* Coleridge (1772-1834) reminds us of the proprietary nature of experience, and laments:

"This is one of the sad conditions of life, that experience is not transmissible. No man will learn from the suffering of another; he must suffer himself. To most men experience is like the stern light of a ship, which illumine only the track it has passed."

Where conformity, obedience and imitation are sponsored, there is competition but never the act of learning, but rather a *"Waiting for orders from headquarters!"* Discipline implies that workers learn, not as it is interpreted for them by specialists, put out in neat little digestible morsels of instruction, but by applying their own complex minds to daily existence. Discipline chisels impressions on the worker's *tabula rasa,* and reflects his uniqueness as a human being.

With discipline, workers learn about each other in relationships, not in conjugal embrace, but in shared intimacies. Discipline breathes life into relationships and resonates with purposeful experience. Disciplined workers are learners, not knowers, flexible and active, not rigid and reactive.

Workers in my experience have inert minds, minds on automatic pilot. They learn by rote, or from a particular person, curriculum, or doctrine; from an exceptional teacher, coach or preacher; or from specific books. They fail, in the main, to learn from their own observations and actions; from their own unique set of life experiences.

The result is that many workers imitate the experience of others. They strive for identity and recognition through conformity, competition and copycatting. They seem unwilling to struggle for identity. The only way true identity and recognition can be achieved is through self-discovery and experience, not by imitating the styles and behaviors of others.

The tremendous burden of attempting to always please others, both personally and professionally, and then to live up to their expectations, has made many workers' minds extraordinarily dull.

After decades of turbulent discord within themselves, festering conflict with others, tiring accommodation, punishing doubt, plus the constant agony of imitation, many workers feel cut off from life, adrift and without anchor.

Through this maddening process of attempting to be like everyone else, many have become second or third-hand persons to themselves. They are always quoting somebody else, never mustering the courage to consider or voice an original thought or opinion. They check pollsters, as if heuristic box scores, to see if they are "thinking right," terrified at the thought they might be outside the prevailing norm. Their consumer choices, dictated by a cadre of experts, compel them to support the "best" films, books, automobiles, neighborhoods, cities, diets, mates, exercises, stocks, *ad infinitum*. Taste is designed by a committee with the lowest common denominator in mind.

When workers are disappointed, they can blame the experts in which they placed their confidence, for the choices were never their own. This reveals an elusive problem. If the choices made are not considered the workers', what chance is there for them to learn from their mistakes? Little or none if *what they are doing is only what they were told to do and little else.*

Identity and recognition thus becomes disingenuous, while actions become clones of someone else's agenda. *Rented minds never act like homeowners.* Alas, I suspect such minds pervade the climate of the home, job, school and community. A poverty of will and a concession to helplessness defines this identity.

Life's hard rule is that everyone is responsible for their own actions, and to learn from the consequences of those actions *everyone gets a report card every day of their lives.*

Workers can be male, female, dark or light, tall or short, fat or trim, young or old, American or Armenian, Indian or Indonesian, life's flow is the same. Movement is similar. Every worker's destiny, whatever it is, depends on observations in school, work, and play and in daily pursuits.

Discipline is not conformity. Discipline involves a mind alert to its own actions — a living mind. Conformity implies conflict between "what is" and "what should be." Conforming to certain prevailing ideologies, social norms and societal "truths," truths to which everyone supposedly subscribes without reflection, seeds conflict.

A discriminating mind cannot absorb what makes little sense. Such a mind must probe and weigh the merits of what is professed against what is experienced. With conflict, there is always friction and the dissipation of energy. Workers can be so absorbed in the conflict that they are not conscious of reality. The result is then confusion.

Each worker must put his own house in order, because no one else is going to do it for him. A mind in disorder gazes at the world through an opaque window, unable to see the beauty and balance of nature. The window holds confusion in and beauty and the enjoyment of other people out.

Workers today are consumed with the distractions of either toys or careers. For them, life is without beauty or order. It is a constant grind, day in and day out. "I work hard and play hard," they proclaim, failing to realize the implicit absurdity in this boast. They have learned the art of moral evasion.

Yet beauty, not wealth or security, is self-generating satisfaction and it is free! The spirit withdrawn into itself and out of sight, may not be completely destroyed, but it could go blind in that internal darkness. What is valued is not always what is precious. As Shakespeare puts it: *"To wilful men, the injuries that they themselves procure must be their schoolmaster."* Indeed!

A paternalistic society knows the value of toys, but not necessarily the essence of beauty. Give a child having a tantrum a mesmerizing toy, and the child is absorbed, distracted from its anguish, and quiet. The child enjoys the mechanics of discovery and is hypnotically involved with the toy. All mischief dissolves.

Society gives workers the toys of technology, the toys of ideals and the toys of beliefs to absorb their discontent. Some toys are treated as sacred (religious doctrine, rites and rituals), others as profane (pop culture), still others as precedence (national holidays).

Tradition as toy assures the maintenance of the company pecking order. No one disputes the CEO's omnipotence. Other toys are status symbols: money, stately homes, expensive automobiles, socio-economic status, knowledge, and so on.

Workers come to venerate ideals, beliefs, policies, customs, norms and hierarchical relationships without reflection. *"It is the way it has always been, so it must be right."* These come to be accepted as "truths," to which the majority subscribe, when they are simply *"Toys of the Mind."*

They are not real. They are fabrications. But when the unreal is treated as real it becomes real in its consequences.

What is appealing about *"Toys of the Mind"* is that we can talk into our machines, into our mobiles (iPhones, smartphones, etc.) and listen to them talk back to us, or delete what appears on our mobiles with a sense of being in control.

Moreover, our mobiles act as an intuitive entity that listens to us, and while giving us this sense of power appears to understand us, and to know us.

We contrive to believe this is true, and even a safe understanding, a privileged relationship tantamount to intimacy, when it is clear that this is the most intrusive device ever invented by man.

That said as denial is nearly as natural to us as breathing, we choose to see our operating systems as manifestations of our consciousness.

We have retreated into the surreal and yet surprised when our lives more resemble a science fiction narrative. The great irony is that our creation, this unnatural hybrid of memory boards and short circuits assembled from the dissecting room of our electronic slaughterhouse has become more human than its human creator. And yet, quite remarkably, we don't seem to be concerned.

"Toys of the Mind" are all inventions of thought and therefore flawed. Even so, some treat these proxies as absolute truths, when there are no such things. There are only a welter of contradictory truths embodied in the worker's imaginary self, a self that is likely

to form his "character." And character is but a mixed bag of relative truths which each worker may call his own.

These psychic toys are proliferating at an alarming rate. Still, they are seldom essential, more apt to be vain accumulations of society's current obsessional aberrations.

These toys are made by man's mind, by man's thought. This doesn't make them any less real, but it does make them more sacrosanct. Psychic toys are now increasingly in the way. But workers have yet to develop a sense of humor about these toys, especially when they are no longer appropriate.

"Toys of the Mind" have their purpose, and that purpose is mostly as distraction. When workers are absorbed in toys, like a child, they are extraordinarily quiet and obedient to the demands of these toys. But take them away and see what happens. You are then messing with their minds, messing with their religion.

These *"Toys"* may be concepts, special interests, or "things." They could be automobiles, boats, houses, planes, athletics, hobbies, but are more than likely the latest electronic wonders. Stated another way, when legitimate tools become obsessional recreational diversions they can approximate the equivalent of a cage of their own making (see *Who Put You in the Cage?* 2015).

Wealth or ambition are also but *"Toys of the Mind"* when they are viewed exclusively in a miser's sense and not in an other-directed sense, in what they can do for others. The list is endless, but the results are always the same. The toys absorb and distract workers from the chaos of "what is," to the appeasing pleasure of selective forgetting.

With effective distraction, there is the absence of self. There is no need to think, experience, problem solve or learn. For the moment, the worker is totally controllable. He differs little with the greyhound at the race track who chases the mechanical rabbit, or the rodent who wanders through the maze for the promised piece of cheese. *The Holy Grail* of this anxious age is the perfect toy to seduce the worker's restless spirit into compliant behavior.

Should the reader think this is a recent challenge, Roman philosopher Seneca (4 B.C. - 65 A.D.) observed: *"Most powerful is he who has himself in his own power. "That* is not likely with the constant subliminal bombardment of distractions.

A QUESTION OF CONTROL!

A violent order is disorder, and a great disorder is an order. These two things are one."
　　　　—**Wallace Stevens**. American modernist poet

THE VERY PROCESS of control breeds disorder just as surely as disorder inevitably leads to control. The more the obsession with control the greater the chaos. Everyone is bound and shaped by control, as control ultimately returns to stabilization and equilibrium. Most workers attempt to control themselves — their tempers, desires, appetites — because it is safe. There is security in control. Control generates a certain sense of safety that with control, that there can be no failure. But, alas, failure is repeated again and again. Why? Our efforts to control become personal. We lose our temper, or are bullied by our passions as slaves to our appetites, while clearly showing an ignorance of the nature of control.

When there is a need for control, chaos is always around the corner. Control manifests a division between the controller and the thing controlled. Virtue does not lie in such separation. This is so because control implies effort, the demand for security, all in the name of what is good. But control is the very denial of goodness, and is therefore disorder. *Does a tree strive for control? Does the universe exert effort to maintain ecological balance? The observer who separates himself from the thing observed is the source of failure, not success.*

A mind which sees directly *within* without the paralysis of analysis is a mind without division. It is a whole mind, a sane mind, a mind one with itself. On the other hand, a neurotic mind is a divided mind, a mind at war with itself, a mind obsessed with control. When such a mind believes it has realized total control, the body cannot move. The person is utterly in the grips of its mania, its neurotic need for control. Such a person is not free, more likely paralyzed with fear, caged in his own obsession.

The neurotic person tells a friend, *"I have an eating disorder. I am a binge eater."* He fluctuates radically in weight from diet and exercise to diet and exercise while between these cycles becomes once again bloated. He thinks admitting his eating disorder is sufficient to dissolve the problem, but it only exacerbates his obsession with food.

Notice how people obsessed with food constantly talk about eating even after having a sumptuous meal.

He has admitted in words *that he has a problem,* but it has not registered on his mind. Therefore, the cycle continues and perhaps even intensifies.

We see this in the artist who is involved in creative destruction. Thought is scrambled from "what is" to what is perceived; integrity of the frame is then restored in one sense and destroyed again in another. This is called "art." The artist, whatever the endeavor, is in the business of control, only that control is then euphemized to an expression of culture.

Control is the basic neurosis of the workplace. Management desires to control workers to ensure that they are productive; that time is not wasted; that the organization operates at maximum efficiency. But do these worthwhile desires materialize? No, because the greater the intensity of management's obsession with control the greater the chaos. The organization is an organism not unlike the autonomic nervous system of the human body, more so now with its electronic connective tissue, and is thwarted from its mission by arbitrary policies and procedures that either deny or take away from this reality.

Control is a function of order, and order is an integral function. Each worker and manager must embody order through their own volition; their own action. Together, worker and manager are one function. What they hold in common is productive work.

George Orwell wrote *"Homage to Catalonia"* (1938) about his personal experience and observations in the Spanish Civil War of the 1930s. Northeastern Spain, more particularly Catalonia, was in the midst of the most far-reaching social revolution seen to that time in Western Europe.

Workers were running factories; peasants, large estates; waiters, restaurants; trolley drivers, complex transport systems; municipal workers, sanitation systems. It didn't last as Fascist General Francisco Franco with the support of Benito Mussolini in Italy and Adolf Hitler in Germany prevailed, but it demonstrated, if only in cameo, what people are capable of doing given the opportunity

The differentiation of managers from workers is an arbitrary one, a division which causes chaos in the world of work. Because of the cultural inclination to separate the controller from the controlled, the analyzer from the analyzed, there is corruption, disorder, distrust, violence and much ruthless manipulation in the workplace. Consequently, the more hysterical the quest for control the greater the workplace paralysis. This is willfully ignored throughout the working world, because control is at war with freedom, when control and freedom are but a single entity.

This is not so with young minds. Such minds are not afraid to learn. They are not yet deeply burdened with knowledge and experience. To learn means to observe oneself without division, without analysis, without denial or the censor of "what should be" and "what should not be." There is no question of control. There is only experience.

Cultural conditioning is anathema to learning, the curse to seeing things clearly, to seeing things as they are. What cultural conditioning promotes is the idea of self-control in the individual, and the appearance of harmony in the workplace, both bogus ideas. This conditioning is the reason there is such madness in society, for the idea of control is the very embodiment of emotional rupture and breakdown.

There is no intrinsic wisdom to self-control. Control is paradoxical. Those consumed with a need for control, lose it, those not bothered with control, have it. What is more appropriate is self-organization, self-order. Workers and managers worry far too much about changing or controlling each other, or other things which disturb them. This is guaranteed to create frustration and conflict, because the only thing workers and managers can change or control is themselves. Order flows from this.

For the past quarter century we have had a bombardment of ideas on how to manage change. Actually, change in the workplace is of only secondary importance. Change will come about naturally, over time, once workers and managers bring about change in themselves. *Order comes from within.* To establish order takes more than good intentions, more than a change in attitude. Order requires a radical change in mentality, a structural change in the way workers and managers view the world. Such radicalism requires the individual *going against the grain.*

As long as there is the analyzer, the supervisor, the director, the administrator feverishly consumed with maintaining order, there will be the problem of chaos. It is such censors who create the problems by failing to understand the dynamics of control.

Unfortunately, as matters now stand, from the moment of birth to the moment of death, workers and managers seem consumed with the need for control of each other. The "must" and "must not," the "should" and "should not" are stenciled on their brains.

This posed little problem when society was moving at a snail's pace. No longer. The world is exploding with people and burgeoning technology Flexibility, not rigidity; creativity, not conformity are now requirements. If anything, less control is called for, thus establishing a climate for the controller and the controlled to merge.

Control has developed a bizarre aspect in this new era of 24/7 cable news programs with journalists as simplifiers and codifiers of complex multi-dimensional conflicts and perturbations across the globe, situations that defy understanding much less explaining.

Yet, these intrepid globe-trotting journalists, such as Thomas Friedman, for instance, jet off to Egypt, Afghanistan, Pakistan, Iraq, and Syria, and a few days later appear on PBS television's Charlie Rose program, and tell us exactly what's wrong, and exactly what those in power should be doing about it, and why they are not. By contrast, the generation of scribes that came out of World War Two, such as Edward R. Murrow, and William L.

Shirer were more circumspect, aware of distortions having seen only a corner of events, and therefore were much less inclined to come off as pundits.

Control implies conformity, imitation, following a particular principle, set of rules, an ideal all the way to respectability. Respectability is a moral dimension which better fits another place and another time. Morality is in the mind of the time, and it changes, not because of some great evil conspiracy, but because the requirements of the times demand it. Respectability cultivates a reverence for "what should be," not "what is," or reality.

Therefore, the very process of control breeds disorder. Disorder is brought about by the censor, the analyzer, the do gooder, the "true believer," the pundit, the one who tries to impose what he thinks is right, instead of qualifying what he is saying or reporting from his limited perspective. Journalists have become "instant historians" in this age of instant everything. The mind of the censor is never a clear mind, capable of candid observation, because such a mind must ferret through various forms of authoritarianism, through vertical hierarchical arrangements, or must gingerly follow some system, guidebook, principle, or form of belief to which it is helplessly tethered. Such a mind does not belong to itself. It is lost to itself, impossibly entangled in the maze of its own stultifying conditioning. Alas, it is the mind of the expert, of the pundit. It is the mind of the times.

The conflict between the controller and the controlled is programmed into workers and managers alike. They are actors in a drama in which they have no creative involvement. Religious and social sanctions control, shape, direct and cement the societal will to its purposes. Jesse Bering calls this *The Belief Instinct* (2011).

Bering asks the question: why is belief so hard to shake? Despite our best attempts to embrace rational thought and reject superstition, we often find ourselves appealing to unseen forces that guide our destiny, wondering who might be watching us as we go about our lives, and imagining what might come after death.

Nancy Reagan, the wife of President Ronald Reagan, and a reputed great influence on his decision-making while president, was fond of consulting an astrologer for guidance. Obviously, she had belief in the relevance of astrology to foretelling events, or why would she be so engaged?

Author Bering unveils the psychological underpinnings of why we believe as we do, shedding light on such topics as our search for a predestined life purpose, our desire to read divine messages into natural disasters and other random occurrences. These include our vision of the afterlife, and our curiosity about how moral and immoral behavior are rewarded or punished in this life.

He traces beliefs and desires to a single trait of human psychology, a "theory of mind," which enables us to guess at the intentions and thoughts of others. He then takes his argument one step further, revealing how the instinct to believe in God and other unknowable forces gave early humans an evolutionary advantage. It gave them the courage to embrace their fears and move forward lifting them out of themselves to grasp the challenges of the unknown and unknowable.

Now such psychological illusions no longer have the same evolutionary cachet. We can't seem to shake our forward inertia. We are slaves to critical thinking, which deals only with what is known, as opposed to creative thinking, which has something in common with our ancestors.

While we are still looking for control outside ourselves, those of our ancient past had no such luxury. It was a matter of survival. This is still the case only it doesn't seem to register the same immediacy.

The controller, whomever he may be, proclaims, "I have the answer!" The answer invariably represents a proposed solution to a fragment of the problem, likely a new fad, gimmick or the rhetoric that provides expedient relief, but seldom a cessation to the aggravation.

The proclaimed answer is tied to the past, to what is known, not to the present or the present situation. It is old knowledge in a new suit of clothes. But reality requires a mind fresh, clear and undivided, a naked mind. Such a mind has no answers, nor does it worry about being offensive, stepping on toes, causing embarrassment, being prohibitively expensive, or fomenting argument. Nor does it worry about acceptance, or *going against the grain.*

On the other hand, most experts reflect minds cluttered with knowledge, with what worked before, or elsewhere. They are lazy minds, impatient minds, the minds of soldiers, enlisted men in officer country, who readily respond to the command, "Get on with it!"

A mind which is one with reality knows it has no answers, no solutions, that all solutions are buried in the problems themselves. But such a revelation does not sell. So, more than likely the solution proposed is a clever, generic idea, simple to understand, comfortable to accept, causing no shift in power, taking the solution's sponsor off the hook, reasonable in cost, and easy to implement. Executives are easily intimidated by thought processes or jargon outside the familiar. Their motto, *"When baffled, it is better to do something than nothing even if it is wrong!"*

A legion of consultants is at the ready to deliver this prescription in canned form with labels still bleeding with the ink of their descriptions to meet the demand. The solution fails in the end, as it must, because each situation is unique and requires great care regarding that fact. The controller and the controlled are integral, inseparable. Still, the "me" and the "not me," the "we" and the "they" strive to divide and control, sustaining disorder. Chaos has a firm grip on enterprise.

Consultants are not the problem. They respond to a need with what will sell. What will sell is "want," not need. Consultants are far better at inventing solutions than perceiving problems. How could it be otherwise? They have limited knowledge of "what is." Moreover, they are outside the process. The solution is always concealed in the problem itself, as certainly as the controller and the controlled are one.

Consultants Thomas Peters and Robert Waterman published *In Search of Excellence* (1982), and companies across the United States rushed to imitate, often to the letter, the precise approach of the profiled companies in the book. Two years later, *Business Week* (November 5, 1984) featured a cover story, "Who's Excellent Now?" More than 50 percent of the companies that established these successful strategies were struggling or failing. It is the state of the inner world of the organization where the key to outer world success resides. In that sense each organization is unique.

It stands to reason, therefore, that the implementing of a system that worked somewhere cannot be expected to work somewhere else, yet that was the frenzied response to this book.

The fallacy of paradigms and success stories is that virtually none of them apply to all situations. Each situation is unique and demands a careful, even proprietary response, preceded of course, by a concise definition of the problem. Defining the problem requires a fresh mind. It takes time to render the mind fit to see clearly "what is" the situation. In other words, you design a way forward. It is an action plan based on a clear understanding of the chronic disturbances of the *inner world* of the organization, and what can be done about these disturbances. You don't search for the answer in the *outer world*; you create it in the *inner world* of the organization.

Generic systems, which is the stock in trade of consultants, are mainly a waste of time, energy and money. They change nothing. The history of generic systems supports this view quite emphatically. What succeeds in one place, fails in another. *Ask Tom Peters*. The difficulty revolves around the neurotic need for the appearance of control, the obsession with focusing on the part at the expense of the whole, and the insistence in seeing workers and managers operating in different universes. But perhaps the fundamental failure is that top management is afraid to get its hands dirty.

In the recent past we have heard much about "re-inventing" and "re-engineering" the corporation, Total Quality Management, Performance Management Systems, and now the *Edenic expectations* of the "information highway." The idea is that the postmodern world is Eden, or paradise, which can be found through man's ingenuity. English philosopher Thomas Carlyle (1795-1881) was weary of this misguided optimism, identifying its aberrational source. He wrote:

> "The machine has gained control not only over the material aspects of society, but also over its philosophy, art and literature. Men have grown mechanical in head and in heart, as well as in hand. Their whole attachments, opinions, turn on Mechanism, and are of a mechanical character."

These mechanistic propositions can easily become toys treated as tools, or little more than distractions, if a holistic approach is not adopted, where cause and effect, the controlled and controller are treated as one.

Control is not a matter of doing something "to the system." It is realized only by a radical change in the mentality of each member of the workforce, where self-order is the outcome. Once movement is made in that direction, it will have a ripple effect, ultimately resulting in a revolutionary restructuring of the culture of the workplace. What deters this is a thinking system that overtly acknowledges change but covertly promotes stability.

Since this dichotomy seems to be in place, is it any wonder that we have little faith in the change process?

To put this in perspective, consider the notion of the implicit social contract, which speaks to workers "vesting" their power in a management team to honor their rights to a pension fund should they retire or be terminated. Workers have granted control of such pension funds on trust (in too many cases) to management teams and/or union consortiums only to find these funds misapplied or depleted due to mismanagement, collusion, or corruption.

As a practical matter, this vesting is not challenged, as power is accumulated like a commodity without opposition. The "conferring" of power makes for the powerful, but what is that? What is "power" and what is "conferring"? Who confers power and how is such conferring done?

Nobody knows. *It is just the way it has always been done!* The conferring is an incomprehensible act. Conferring power, acquiring power, using power, is what workers surrendered as if on automatic pilot. Workers everywhere remain in the dark: *obscurum per obscurius*. All they know is that power is another word for control, and in their experience such control has always been outside their experience.

What currently worries workers is that those in charge, the CEOs and their courtiers, are not always diligent.

Events have proven to be the master. It is not uncommon that workers in the trenches have a better feel for the "state of the company." It can even be argued that decisions issued in the trenches are likely to seem crucial in retrospect. Perfectly sensible orders issued from mahogany row may prove ultimately an embarrassment, foiled by an unfavorable work climate or the turn of events.

Power (control) exercised in the wrong place at the wrong time, and in the wrong manner invariably leads to corporate derailment or the equivalent of a corporate train wreck. Stated another way, internal organizational stress and strain, if not acknowledged and properly addressed, can lead to organizational fatigue and instability, and consequently, an inability to respond effectively to accelerating external competitive demands.

Alexis de Tocqueville's 19th century, *Democracy in America* (1834-1836), expressed anxiety about the pervasiveness of "soft despotism" in the conduct of business. His insight turned prophetic in the 20th century as we saw management attempting, and largely succeeding, to kill trade unionism with kindness. Its success has contributed to an undesirable outcome, worker disenfranchisement. This destabilization has led to worker cynicism, apathy, and counter dependence.

Unwittingly, management's disingenuous approach to power sharing has led to workers going from being management dependent to being counter dependent on the organization for their total well-being, placing workers and managers poles apart.

Much energy is wasted at this interface. Managers with position power become aggressive, while workers with knowledge power retreat into submissive passive behaviors. Line managers know about this situation, but are far removed from corporate decision-makers.

Meanwhile, first causes are accessible to trench workers, who experience them first hand. If acted upon immediately, crises can be avoided later.

But workers too often do not act. They wait for orders from above. Control of the situation, when it is controllable, slips out of control and into a major crisis. This alone, and nothing deeper or more interesting, is the source of common corporate perturbations.

To be fair, managers have gravitated to a role as have workers that has proven counterproductive. Managers would rather take the blame for disasters than admit impotence in the face of events. Prudent decision making is a necessary as well as sufficient condition of the joint problem solving, especially in this electronic age.

Traditional executive leadership is a luxury workers can no longer afford. They must take charge of their lives and destinies. For workers to enjoy the fruits of their labors they must accept an equal share of the responsibilities. This requires commitment and accountability, and the ability to take risks and failure in stride. It requires mature adult workers.

Once established, there will be a different working mentality and a radically different distribution of power. No grand design will produce this outcome. It will be a gradual process based upon the primal drive of workers, survival!

The focus will shift from disorder to order. Power will begin to flow organically according to demands of the task; decisions will be made at the level of consequences; managers and workers will be treated as teammates; management will be part of the workforce, as compensation and entitlements will be brought more in line. Mythic executive infallible authority will vanish. Interdependency will be the key to order.

CONTROL & ENVY

To grasp this concept, consider control on a personal basis. If a worker is "envious," he is told he must control his envy. This is wrong. This tends to separate envy from the person. He says, "I must not be envious!" This never works, as he becomes more obsessed with what others have and are than ever before.

The worker is not separate from envy. He is envy! There is no way to change that fact. He may try to control envy as though it was separate from him, but it cannot be done. He may attempt to imitate someone else who has mastered his envy, and this, too, will fail. Not until he embraces the fact that envy is integral to his nature, can envy be understood, and therefore controlled.

The worker, who deals successfully with envy, moves toward envy, not away from it. He admits to himself that envy is "what is," that he is the cause and effect of his own condition. This allows him to deal with his envy by bringing all the pain to the surface. Envy no longer is buried in his mind where it gnaws at him. Subject and object are one. Envy is controlled. He no longer feels a need to control envy, so he can. Without cause, there is no effect.

Once he accepts envy as part of his nature, part of his character, he has come to accept himself as he is, and is on his way to accepting others as he finds them.

On the other hand, look at the 1960s and the *Sexual Freedom Revolution*. More than five decades later, sex is obsessional and more, not less a problem. Ask yourself, are we, as a society, more or less attuned to our sexual nature? Do we have more or fewer psycho-sexual hang-ups?

Human sexuality in the 1960s became a thing apart from the person. Sexuality became divorced from love, and even lust, to become objectified to people behaving like thrashing about objects, no longer persons. This led to exponential expansion of the pornography industry and all its social sexual implications. Human sexuality became this terrible mystery that needed to be sorted out.

Sexuality was treated as a beast which needed to be released from its cage, or society would go mad (cause). The mystery was not solved, but the beast was released. Once out of its cage, it leaped into another, the cage of sexual aberration. The mind became the enemy of the body, the natural perverted. Society submersed itself in sexual frenzy (effect), chasing the ultimate orgasm. This frenzy invaded all aspects of life.

Hedonism as therapy became the laboratory of experience in the 1950s orchestrated by Hugh Hefner (born 1926), among others, a playboy mentality at the controls. William Masters and Virginia Johnson, a generation later, wrote *"Human Sexual Response"* (1966), creating a whole new industry. Far from providing insight into the problem, they unwittingly spiked it, leading to a rash of sexually-transmitted diseases, escalating divorce, mental anxiety, and in some cases suicide and homicide.

Erotic junkies sold lust as love, pleasure as purpose, and greed as good. Copulation became a form of competence, more esteemed than caring. Sexual parlor games became the new religion. No one confessed to continence for it was an embarrassment to be chaste. Four letter words became the code of belonging, and no one would be caught dead admitting to being totally straight.

In the wake of the sexual revolution we have an epidemic of AIDS, a rampant problem of teenage suicides, a plague in substance abuse, a scandalous increase in physical and psychological abuse, an atrocious increase in teenage pregnancies, with an upsurge in both abortions and illegitimacy. So, the question to ask is, can workers live their lives without a single control? Can anyone live a life, which is at present so disastrous, so mechanical, so repetitive, so calloused and chaotic, without a single control? The answer is, not likely.

Freedom from attachment can only happen when the mind is free; when the mind is still; when the mind gives complete attention to quiet; when the mind learns to live within the bounds of its limits, without the conflict that arises from control; when the mind puts aside its conditioning and sees the world "as it is"; when the mind and body are a single whole; when the mind accepts that the controller and the controlled are one; when the mind embraces its problems rather than apologizes for them; when the mind prefers order to chaos.

ATTENTION VERSUS CONCENTRATION

On balance, however, problems seem to become progressively worse the more we consider them. Why? Workers confuse attention with concentration. Attention and concentration are qualitatively different.

Most of us know what *concentration* is. Societal conditioning grooves our minds to concentrate at school, in sport and throughout our professional life. Workers are constantly told that they need to concentrate more. Wrong!

To concentrate implies bringing all energy to a single focus. But thought invariably intervenes and the mind wanders away from the focus. A perpetual battle then ensues between the desire to concentrate and the restless mind's desire to wander, and resist control. The conflict is merciless.

Attention has no control, no concentration. It is complete attention. This means all energies and capacities — mind, heart and soul — are given to attention. Few ever experience complete attention. If they do, there is no record of the attending, no action from memory. The mind does not record. It observes only. Whereas when concentrating, when making an effort, one acts from memory. Memory plays back old mental tapes and films — horror tales of "what was," or "what should have been." These memories get in the way of attention, in the way of seeing things clearly. Since attention is difficult, the mind is more likely to take a bypass to the more accessible mechanism of concentration, and so the vicious cycle continues.

With the mind, there is no need to record, except that which is necessary to get through daily life. Yet our minds are occupied, never still, filled continuously with fragments of thought. A busy mind is not a thoughtful mind. It is a spastic mind.

To learn how to observe, to see "what is," requires the freedom to observe. Most workers are disinclined to embrace such a challenge. They fill their heads instead with nonsense. It is not necessary to be saturated with useless psychological recordings, either of insults or flattery, compulsive worries or "might have beens."

When one sees the futility of recording nonsense, the mind is free from its conditioning. It has removed its rose colored glasses. Most workers, sad to say, appear slaves to memory, slaves to taking seriously what others think of them, what others say about them, slaves to their failures and embarrassments.

Workers are programmed to believe they are different from each other; that successful workers are different from failures, and both are different from themselves. They are not. Alas, the very highest and lowest are painfully similar.

Workers are conditioned to being threatened by diversity. Yet all workers are more alike than different, for they have the same kinds of minds, and go through the same miseries and joys, the same happiness and sorrow, shed the same kinds of tears, and experience the same euphoria and elation when they achieve success together.

To comprehend this, the mind must be free to consider data which may not necessarily fit with what is already there. This takes courage. It demonstrates the need for workers to stand alone, and accept their isolation, before they can stand together. Most workers are afraid of this detachment, so the herd mentality wins their minds.

Such workers cling to others just like themselves, eternally chattering without saying anything, preoccupied with one thing or another, without being in charge. It is only the silent mind, the mind that is free, the mind that is not afraid to stand alone, that can see into "what is" and exercise control without the need to be in control.

WHY EMBRACING A PARADIGM SHIFT IS SO RARE

"The man who embraces a new paradigm at an early stage must often do so in defiance of the evidence provided by the problem solving."

—Thomas S. Kuhn,
American physicist, historian, and philosopher of science

THERE IS a discernible contrast between the reality of the worker's life today and its historical antecedence. The worker is at once a collection of atoms living its own conscious life "for itself," and at the same time the unconscious agent of change often despite itself. Since workers are not, in fact, free, but could not live without the conviction that they are, it is better that they understand what goes on as they do, than to seek to subvert such common sense beliefs.

"Happy ignorance" rules the head if not the heart of most workers. Even so, there is movement against the grain, now a slight tremor but rapidly building. The focus of this natural fault line is apparent — *The Ascent of the Working Woman!*

"Great men" do not move workers from their epicenter, but "important people" do appear when discontinuity leads to shock waves of catastrophe. These people are less important than they may suppose, but neither are they shadows. They embody the strengths and weaknesses, the passions and dreams, the nightmares and madness of their times. They step out of the darkness and display wisdom. They appear when rhetoric is reduced to rubble. Wisdom is not a matter of pedigree or credentials, not a matter of accumulated knowledge or experience, wisdom is a way of thinking creatively unencumbered with the known or with what has worked before.

> Given this, the deciding factor when it comes to going against the grain takes courage. Evidence of this courage was displayed by professional baseball player, Curtis Flood when he sued Major League Baseball for the right to collective bargain for himself.

When Flood came to Marvin Miller, Director of the Players Association of Major League Baseball, he could see the athlete's mind was made up. *"I told him,"* recalls Miller, *"that given the courts' history of bias toward the owners and their monopoly, he didn't have a chance in hell of winning.*

"More important than that, I told him even if he won, he'd never get anything out of it—he'd never get a job in baseball again."

Flood asked Miller if it would benefit other players. *"I told him, yes, and those to come."* He said, *"Then let's do it!"*

Flood won, he was, as Miller predicted out of baseball, and professional athletes have been basking in Flood's courage ever since.

THE TANGLED WEB OF RELIGION, SCIENCE, HISTORY AND CHANGE

To put this in perspective, permit this brief excursion. The working man's faith in ideas has controlled his lot far more than he might believe. Belief is the most powerful motivator known to man.

In the Western world, workers once had a deep commitment to an ancient faith, Roman Catholicism. That faith has eroded in the last 500 years, with some insisting workers have become amoral. Closer to the truth, workers have changed. They have adapted to stress and accelerating demands not always wisely perhaps, but inevitably. Change is never born in the void.

Religion for centuries played its part in the persistent pursuit of the spiritual truth treating secular truth as if the enemy as specialization became increasingly dominant, which required people to be educated and enlightened and to live in the "now" as opposed to a focus on the hereafter.

The Church argued it, alone, understood the "inner rhythms," the silent march of things. Only those who understood this "truth" knew what could or could not be achieved, what should or should not be attempted. The "Doctors of the Church" believed they alone held the key to secular success as well as spiritual salvation. Omniscience belonged to God alone, and they were His agents. Only by immersing ourselves in His Word dare we hope for wisdom.

Against this cultural inculcation, another truth emerged, empirical or practical wisdom. This is knowledge of the inevitable: of what, given the symmetry of Mother Nature, could not but happen; or conversely, of how things cannot be, or could not have been. The rare capacity for seeing this we call a "sense of reality." This has been the domain of science and the scientist.

There is a lack of empathy for religious believers today in the United States, especially among young people, the so-called "millennials." They see people of faith as judgmental, hypocritical, old-fashioned, or simply out of touch, according to social commentator David Brooks. Yet, between the doubters and the believers, Brook's writes,

> *"There is a silent majority who experience a faith that is attractively marked by combinations of fervor and doubt, clarity and confusion, empathy and demand."*

Why should it be any different for faith? Is this not the age of ambivalence? Spiritual and secular truth, truths of the heart and mind, spirit and reason, religion and science, have been warring with each other for centuries. Men of God insist the human intellect is but a feeble instrument when pitted against the power of divine forces; that rational explanations of human conduct seldom explain anything. Secular truths are inadequate if only because they ignore man's "inner" experience. A high value is set on family life and on the superiority of the heart over the head, the moral over the intellect. Notice that as economics evolved to competition as opposed to cooperation and theology devolved to science, the heart and the head no longer experienced comfort in the same body.

By the curious supposition of secular humanists that the 21st century represents *life after faith,* the rhetoric used continues to sound less like liberation and more like defeat.

It would seem that the language humanists choose to use betrays their emotional agenda as the talk centers on the "death of God" and the "loss of faith," and not on the rebirth of reason and the enlightening achievement of truth.

Read Voltaire or Friedrich Nietzsche, Christopher Hitchens or Sam Harris and you will find ethical, philosophical and scientific arguments against faith, belief and religion, but little clarity on what these humanists advocate.

Political science scholar Michael Walzer in *The Paradox of Liberation: Secular Revolutions and Religious Counterrevolutions* (2015) argues that to summarily reject the religious specter is to be haunted by counterrevolution.

He asks the question, why do secular revolutions beget these counter religious revolutions? What is there about religion that critics of religion fail to understand about these movements?

The book examines what befell Ben-Gurion's vision in Israel, Jawaharlal Nehru's in India and Ahmed Ben Bella's in Algeria.

Men of science stand apart. They hold that only by patient empirical observation can reliable knowledge be obtained; that this knowledge, even then, is always inadequate and incomplete, but that it must be sought.

The solitary thinker draws a gloomy picture of the impotence of the human will against the rigid laws of the universe. Yet men of science display the same vanity of human passion as they attempt to uncover its mysteries, while failing to comprehend much less explain the bases of their irrational actions and feelings. They aspire to reduce man to a manageable lot, to a condition of predictability, where passionless man can no longer be frustrated, humiliated or wounded. Men of science have a near metaphysical belief in logical detachment, whereas the religious have an equally metaphysical belief in supernatural detachment.

Doctors of the church and men of science represent the spiritual and secular half of the same whole. Both long for a universal explanatory principle, composed of the bits and pieces of the furniture of the universe, which may be reduced to a single unifying design. From their respective vantage points, the quest for a unifying theory of the universe and a quest for the *"HOLY GRAIL"* appear to be equally elusive.

They are men, like all working men, and therefore their personal and professional lives are an inescapably tangled web of unresolved issues, conflicts and savage battles between their gifts as thinkers and their passionate ideals; between what they are and what they purport to be. If you have any doubt how human men and women of science are, read Brenda Maddox's *"Rosalind Franklin: The Dark Lady of DNA"* (2002) and *"The Double Helix"* (1968) by James Watson.

The humanness of scientists is illustrated by Mario Livio's *"Brilliant Blunders"* (2014), where he traces the great scientific blunders of such leading lights as Charles Darwin, Lord Kelvin, Linus Pauling, Fred Hoyle and Albert Einstein, all of whom are known for their great discoveries.

David Lindberg and Ronald Numbers in *"When Science & Christianity Meet"* (2003) ask the question:

Have science and Christianity been locked in moral combat for the past 2,000 years, or has their relationship been one of conscious coexistence, encouragement and support?

Both views have been vigorously defended, and both have been rejected as oversimplification of the clearly palpable human conflict between faith and reason, fact and value, the irrational longing for immortality and the rational seeking reality coherence.

Christianity bridges existence with a focus outside of time whereas the focus of science, in contrast, is within the limits of time.

Science consists of facts and theories, which are born in different ways. Facts are true or false, which are discovered through experimentation, whereas theories are free associations of facts and fantasies, creations of the human mind, intended to describe our understanding of nature, or in my case, human nature. Theories are tools and need not be precisely true in order to be useful. It is easy to argue against theories based upon one's own experience, but it is much more difficult to argue against facts, which in science can be replicated and therefore corroborated.

At no time in history has there been such a gathering of scientists with such powers of insight — with the uncanny ability to probe and differentiate — as now, and yet, on balance, never have so many displayed such profound ignorance! Society is lost because too often theories are treated as facts by scientists as well as laymen, which is unfortunate. Einstein concurs. He writes, *"The more one chases after the quanta, the better they hide themselves."*

Could it be that man seeks too much, that he overestimates his capacities? If only the most gifted of men displayed a little humility and realized that conflict is natural and harmony artificial, and paradise on earth is not the absence of struggle but its requisite.

From the beginning of recorded history, workers have struggled to find truth, failing to realize truth, outside of nature, is relative. What is truth to you may not be truth to me. Religion has been at the forefront to carry workers on this journey. This has unwittingly devolved and turned intimacy into contractual matters to be litigated. David Brooks writes:

"There must be something legalistic in the human makeup, because cold, rigid unambiguous, unparadoxical belief is common, especially considering how fervently the scriptures oppose it."

Religion and science combine to be "apostles of despair." Both speak with the same angry irony, both are deeply skeptical of each other's powers. They have lost faith with faith.

Organized religions seem hardly religious, struggling as it does to remain relevant, while somehow being thrown off stride by dynamic progressive change, while man, himself, has essentially not changed at all, and therefore needs what religion has always provided, which is sanctuary from contemporary madness.

Could the cause be our dwindling religious inheritance over the last two centuries that accounts for the gradual disintegration of one's spiritual education as the guiding force to a life ideal?

Is Dostoyevsky's novel, *The Brothers Karamazov (1880)* representative of a universe of growing tragedy and depravity in which evil and suffering are not eradicable accidents but deeply woven into the texture of our being?

Religious leaders appear fainthearted warriors. They fail to see that spiritual need (theology) and secular demand (science) are complementary forces. Einstein put it succinctly, *"Science without religion is tame, religion without science is blind."*

The clergy seem less certain of their role in postmodern society than the average worker does of his. A disconnect between the clergy and church goers has resulted.

Could it be that the church is more interested in its survival than its mission, more a financial institution of fiscal fiduciary relevance rather than a sanctuary for troubled or bankrupt souls?

Faith and money are at the core of all religious institutions. Although faith can exist without money, religious institutions cannot.

The New Testament claims that Jesus proclaimed the coming of the celestial kingdom, but it was the church that actually arrived.

When illiteracy was the norm in Europe through the first thousand years of the Christian era, magnificent cathedrals were built to capture the imagination of the faithful in compensation for pervasive illiteracy. The clergy reign supreme even over monarchs and princes.

With Gutenberg's invention (15th century) of movable type in printing, followed by Martin Luther's translation of the Bible, (16th century) literacy spread like a rash across Europe. The Bible was translated into indigenous languages, literacy flourished, and common cultures were born. Feudalism and the peasant class was eroding, while capitalism and a market economy was driving people off the land and into factories and crowded cities.

Nation states evolved as national cultures grew out of common languages and values. Kingdoms and empires became disenchanted with the temporal authority of the Church. Meanwhile, the *Catholic collective conscience of feudalism* was now threatened with the *Protestant individualistic conscience of capitalism.*

This led to breakaway sects such as the *Puritans* (17th century) who left their known European society to embrace the unknown in the New World in order to freely practice their faith. A new society was taking root on the American continent.

The *American and French Revolution* (late 18th century) were fought in quest of individual political freedom, and economic and social justice. America had a series of wars with Great Britain, but ultimately established a republic as a constitutional democracy and a new nation-state. The French went through a *Reign of Terror* following the French Revolution, and experienced great instability.

Stepping into that instability was Napoleon Bonaparte, declaring himself Emperor, placing the crown on his own head instead of leaving that ceremony, and all that it symbolized, to the Supreme Pontiff of Holy Mother Church. The *Napoleonic Wars* (early 19th century) followed until a confederacy of European nations defeated him at Waterloo in Belgium. Fifty years later, the *American Civil War* (late 19th century) led to the *Emancipation Proclamation,* liberating Negro slaves from bondage, and inaugurating the *Industrial Revolution.* Factories, machines, steel mills, railroads and a plethora of inventions signaled a new day. It also marked the rise of the secular and decline of the spiritual. German philosopher Friedrich Nietzsche's madman captured this sentiment with his statement, *"God is dead!" God* wasn't dead. He just changed His uniform.

Believers simply moved away from religious doctrine to a secular belief system placing a higher value on the materialistic ritual of career than on the spiritual tenets of religion.

This proved as true for Catholics as Protestants. Moreover, pervasive materialism called for the reconfiguring of Jesus' promise of treasure in Heaven not only by equating it with treasure on earth, but by marginalizing the original notion that money should go to the poor as a means of assuring prayerful intercession with those who had gone before.

An obsession with acquisitiveness (i.e., wealth and property) would prove the perfect prescription for gratuitous violence.

Nietzsche died (1900) in the dawn of the 20th century, the most violent century in the history of man with WVVI, WWII, the atomic bombing of Japan, the annihilation of six million Jews, the Korean War, Vietnam War, and a number of other wars across the globe.

The *Austro-Hungarian* and *Persian* empires were split up. The draconian reparation demands of the *Versailles Peace Treaty* after WWI were so extreme that they opened the door to Adolf Hitler and Nazis Germany, and WWII.

An explosion in technology followed WWII, including space exploration, and the boilerplate for the *Information Age* (21st century), which has become inadvertently an anxious age, an unconscious age, and an age seemingly in total retreat from the spiritual self. This has resulted in man's self-estrangement, making him less the master of his fate and more its pawn. Rather than find a new connection with these iterative changes, the Church has relegated itself to the role of ritualistic entertainer, which has left man sensing abandonment.

Religion as distraction has continued to foster the "should be" qualities worshippers' desire. There is a certain irony to this, a manifest dishonesty and deception. It is an expedient design. It has not always been so.

Religion had vitality in the 16th century when a single cleric, Martin Luther, went against the grain of the dominant figure of the culture of the time, The Holy See of Rome, His Holiness, Pope Leo X, to post his 95 theses on the door of the Wittenberg chapel. This was unprecedented. Here a young cleric was putting his career and comfort in jeopardy for what he believed. He had little support, and was immediately labeled a heretic. Some called him a madman, pointing out the emotional character to his temperament. He was all alone. He made no apology for his act as he believed his regeneration could only come from within, and that the source of that inner life was concealed in his immortal soul.

The enormity of this act is difficult to comprehend today. Clearly, it was not motivated by self-interest, or to justify disobedience to the Holy See. It was an act of conscience and conviction, not deviance, an act with a complete willingness to accept the consequences. As an individual, he stepped outside the obedient rank and file and declared himself one with his Creator.

Scripture revealed to Luther a loving God, not the God he was programmed to worship. This loving God bestowed on sinful man the free gift of salvation through faith alone. The church's liturgical dogma necessitating good works to attain salvation was revoked. Luther's theology went against the grain of accepted Roman Catholic teaching, and cut to the core the hypocritical practice of selling indulgences.

Earning indulgences was proclaimed as a way to avoid Purgatory, and to go straight to heaven upon death. Indulgences were created originally to award believers for their good works. But the affluent, who had little time or felt little inclination to do good works, bypassed the process by buying indulgences.

Indulgences were sold wholesale the way scalpers sell tickets to rock concerts today. The practice was ludicrous, but no one did anything.

The Roman Catholic Church was the most powerful force in Western Europe, indeed, in most of the civilized world. It condoned the practice of selling indulgences presenting a blind eye to the activity until one man, Martin Luther, demonstrated the courage to take on the entire Roman Catholic establishment, by going against the grain.

With that single heroic act, Luther set the chain reaction which would release the worker from "The Dark Ages" of corporate dependency on Holy Mother Church, and plant the seeds for a growing individualism. Western man's mindset and disposition was thus to undergo radical restructuring.

What is most remarkable about this is that Martin Luther was not a saint, not cast in the mold of the "great man," not even an especially "learned man," a man with many of the psycho-sexual flaws of modern man, a man who made the same foot prints as his contemporaries. He was neither a demigod nor a scoundrel, only a man of intense passion and focus. But he was a man of substance whereas shallowness ruled his day as it does ours.

As with workers today, Luther's contemporaries immersed themselves in the medium of the mundane. Life was taken for granted with the many living in feudalistic dependence on the church, which was quite corrupt at the time, dictating the terms of that dependency.

When other-directed, the individual fails to see the absurdity of his dependence. His consciousness is so clearly interwoven with the flow of things that he cannot separate himself from them or their demands.

When workers are caged in standards of truth and falsehood, of reality and the ideal, of the good and the bad, of the central and the peripheral, of the subjective and objective, of the beautiful and the ugly, of movement and rest, of past, present and future, of one and the many, they are kin to the time of Martin Luther. These are the basic presuppositions of man throughout the ages.

Martin Luther could not analyze his predicament from an external vantage point because with change there is only inner resolution. So, the question might be asked, was Luther more conscious of his times than his contemporaries as change agent? My sense is that he was not, that is, until he visited Rome and saw the corruption first hand. The posting of his 95 theses on his Wittenberg Church door on October 31, 1517, was to my mind an impulsive act consistent with his temperament, a way of atoning for his raging mood swings.

The superficial dominates every age and masks the disturbing tremors few acknowledge until they are shocked into awareness.

Wisdom abhors the superficial. It burrows through "the way things are." Wisdom is not scientific, but a sensitivity to the circumstances of the times. It is felt!

Wisdom is more apt to be displayed by the mind of the peasant than the aristocrat, a mind that looks for simple truths and is not blindsided by the profound allegiance to the status quo. Neither the rules of science nor religion need necessarily apply, but rather the inescapable sense of justice. Martin Luther was in that sense, wise. He was an honest man, and an honest man has the gift of clarity.

His protest led to the establishment of *Protestantism* and a new identity for the worker. The worker would come to see his relationship to himself, his Creator and to his world in more accountable terms. Holy Mother Church lost a dependent.

John Calvin, the French theologian, was even bolder. He established the *Protestant Ethic,* which drew a marked distinction between the saved and the damned. Personal salvation, he professed, is tied to energetic pursuit of health, wealth and happiness to the honor and glory of God. Accomplishment in this life is not only important, but is indicative of *"The Elect,"* or *"The Chosen."*

Believers demonstrate the right to that status by their success, which is seen as a measure of God's grace. The man of property, not poverty is thus the embodiment of the man of God.

The fatalism of Catholicism was set aside. There was no honor in playing the victim, or celebrating humility. Individualism displayed in public works enjoyed a new dignity, success a new prominence. The need for a priest as intercessor in Holy Confession became unnecessary. Calvinism, as with Lutheranism before, taught that salvation is a pure gift from God, and cannot be earned.

Out of this came the *Protestant Work Ethic,* which advocated self-discipline, self-reliance, self-examination, hard work and dedication to duty. Capitalism was secure. Sociologist Max Weber (1864 - 1920) captured the essence of this in his book, *The Protestant Ethic and the Spirit of Capitalism* (1905).

In going against the grain, Western man has set the pace for prosperity over the past 500 years. This tradition is now eroding. The religious motivation, which inspired this radical departure from conventional thinking, is all but gone. Modern religion goes with, not against the grain of the prevailing norm. Religion has lost its moral compass and calling. Roman Catholicism is no longer its curse, but science. Religion cowers before science and imitates its deficiencies. There appear no Martin Luthers or John Calvins on the horizon.

Workers in my experience have scant acquaintance with the *Protestant Work Ethic.* Nor do these workers subscribe to the philosophy of systematic profits through hard work, thrift and the reinvestment of earnings — basic characteristics of early capitalism. They play the Lotto, are habitual river boat gamblers, frequent state sponsored casinos (which are springing up like convenient stores), or look to inherit.

Increasingly, conventional behavior is driven more by luck than pluck. Going against the grain is an anomaly. *Mature adult workers* are in short supply. The mind of mature adult workers is:

A mind which is free from vain attachments, from foolish conclusions and concepts. It deals only with what is, not with what should be, or might be "with a little luck." Such a mind is impatient with societal excess.

A mind not sympathetic to patronage, benign or otherwise. The tyranny of "top-down authority" is no longer acceptable. But bottom-up control is still a fantasy, because few have the courage to go against the grain.

A mind involved in everyday life, and with what happens, both outwardly and inwardly, such a mind wants to deal with problems on the basis of reality, not on the basis of "what should be. "With such a mind, there is little room for denial or delay.

A mind free of denominational, racial, national, ethnic and socioeconomic prejudices, it is a mind also beyond tradition, beyond cultural inculcation, and historical direction. Its redemption is found in getting beyond partisan gridlock, the paralysis of analysis, to deal effectively with the possible.

One comforting thought is that if Martin Luther had not come forward, someone else would have made the breakthrough. When society is ready, its conscience surfaces.

Luther was a ponderer, who could not avoid seeing what he saw and remain unmoved. Yet his ambivalent spirit had to be shocked into action. The trigger was a trip to Rome where he saw how extensive church corruption. He was torn between his Christian God and death, as historian Richard Marius puts it in his dazzling portrait of the monk *(Martin Luther,* 1999). Alas, Luther was neither more saint nor less sinner than his contemporaries, and struggled with depression all his life.

Earlier (see Preface) mention was made that depressives

seem more in touch with reality. We live in an age fearful of depression. Luther was not afraid of his depression, but embraced it, and because of that, his truth touched the silent cords of his tacit generation, which had no language to describe, much less face its doubt.

Clarity of mind is assumed as necessary in the pursuit of truth. But what is truth, and whose truth is being sought? Is it absolute truth?

Were that the case, in retrospect, Martin Luther would be a divine, which he clearly wasn't.

Luther was stunned by church corruption, and stumbled on the miscarriage of justice as well as truth denied, picked himself up, probably saying, "This is not right! Indeed, this is wrong!"

By doing so, then by struggling to comprehend what it all meant, he made his struggle for clarity that of other disillusioned German Catholics, and the rest is history. Had that not occurred, history would have ignored him.

Certainty is personal, not objective, and everyone has a right to their own certainty. The mind of mature adult workers knows and accepts this. Such minds, however, currently go quietly about their duties with little inclination to go against the grain. They lack the passion, perhaps the maddening conviction of Martin Luther, and so we wait for the mature adult worker to personify a more appropriate mentality. Such a person will not be certain his truth will win the day. He does so because he must. As Thomas Kuhn adds:

"He must have faith that the new paradigm will succeed with the many large problems that confront it knowing only that the older paradigm has failed with a few. A decision of that kind can only be made on faith."

EMPIRICAL EVIDENCE OF THIS DRAMATIC SHIFT

A CAREER-CHANGING PERSONAL BRIEF

"If conscience smite these once, it is an admonition; if twice, it is a condemnation. What other dungeon is so dark as one's own heart! What jailer as inexorable as one's own self!"

—**Nathaniel Hawthorne** (1804-1864), American novelist

JUST AS GOING along to get along may be natural to most people, going against the predominant grain is equally as inherent as breathing for others. This seems to have been the case with the Major League baseball player, Curtis Flood, as it was for the German Roman Catholic cleric, Martin Luther. It was also true for this author.

Taking a stand is visceral. It involves having a center and a moral compass that says the prevailing norms are wrong. Such a position often defies reason and good sense as its costs are quickly apparent.

Consequently, going against the grain is not for everyone. For those so predisposed, there is no other recourse. They have to act to live with themselves.

While it may be self-defining, it is invariably at the expense of self-alienation from the herd. Such ostracism may be as selective as social Darwinism.

In 1958, I left the R&D laboratory as a chemist at Standard Brands, Inc., and joined Nalco Chemical Company as a chemical sales engineer, never having sold anything before. Two weeks in the field after a month of training at the home office in Chicago, I was told I was not cut out for this kind of work.

I had offended the area manager by answering his question: What have you learned after traveling with me for two weeks? I told him nothing as he never ask for an order, never listened to customers, never found out what they needed, and mainly wasted their time and ours socializing.

This resulted in my being given marginal accounts to service, and the right to call on competitors, but for only six weeks after which time I was to find other employment.

During that painful period, however, I sold the largest account of the district's operation in years — taking it from a major competitor — by listening, asking what the customer needed, and was not getting, while working closely with engineering and operations as a partner, an advocate, not as an adversary.

Nalco would send 78 sales engineers (yes, I kept track) from other districts to work with me. They also ask me to make presentations at various Nalco conclaves across the country to share my approach to selling technical systems to highly savvy prospects, as the word was out that Fisher doesn't sell "technically"!

Such opportunities gave me corporate exposure and a chance to capture my ideas on paper. This led to rapid promotion and elevated me to executive status in the international division when barely thirty.

The momentous ride found me working in South America, Europe and finally facilitating the creation of a new company in South Africa. It was there I hit a wall, that is, South Africa apartheid.

This clashed with my values and a reality foreign to my cultural programming.

At the top of my career, father of four young children, in my mid-thirties, I resigned from Nalco, resettled in Florida, wrote a book, did little else for two years but read books, play tennis, and attempt, however unsuccessfully, to write for a living.

When nearly broke, I went back to school full-time, year around, to earn a Ph.D. in industrial-organizational psychology, consulting on the side.

Once I had my Ph.D., I joined one of my clients, Honeywell, Inc., as an organizational development (OD) psychologist, which proved a repeat of the Nalco experience. Having been a free-wheeling line executive, it was a new experience to be relegated to an "in house" staff function in human resources of a large facility (4,000 employees) on a scenic campus in sunny South Florida, and expected to echo the company line without variance, or else!

Not known to be a policy wonk, it came as no surprise that the human resource director suggested shortly after my settling in, *"We don't believe you're cut out for this kind of work,"* while my OD boss stated more accurately, *"Find your role here in the next few weeks or you'll be gone!"*

A clinical psychologist deals with an individual client and addresses problems in terms of behavior. An OD psychologist deals with the organization as his client and addresses performance problems in terms of workers and managers in the workplace. He exercises no bias towards either group, as he attempts to observe them unobtrusively in action.

My approach to OD was as eccentric as my methodology had been in selling. I met with groups not as an expert or with an agenda, but with a desire to find out what got in the way of their productive efforts and what they, as a group, thought needed to be done.

At first, I was distrusted, then challenged, then accepted as the real deal and a breath of fresh air. For Honeywell to have gotten rid of me, then, might have caused a protest, as rank and file workers, professionals and blue collars alike, were not used to being taken seriously, or to have their best interests taken to heart.

Honeywell groups asked me to give speeches to various technical and professional associations, while for management, I wrote monographs, presented papers and gave speeches to technical conferences, and made interventions based on worker consensus ideas, one of which was the creation of an "in house" technical education program to address systemic deficiencies.

The director of the Charles Stark Draper Laboratories at Massachusetts Institute of Technology, read one of these publications, and invited me to Cambridge to work with CSDL's designing team for the ring laser gyros being manufactured at Honeywell Avionics facility in Clearwater, Florida.

So, it wasn't unusual for the Department of Contracts Administration Services (DCAS) to approach me in 1984 to give the keynote speech at a department sponsored conference on *Participative Management,* when that theme was the flavor of the month across corporate America.

Having given "offsite" seminars for this group before, I felt it necessary to make clear my reservations about "Participation Management," asking to be allowed to be critical of the value of this intervention. The selecting committee said in unison, "No problem!"

That proved to be in error. My speech became a major problem, for me, as I explain in the segment, "Going against the Grain."

This was 1984. My manager, a very capable man understood OD, and granted me creative license to practice the discipline. In a subsequent segment *(A Typology of Leaderless Leadership),* he might best be described as the "Happily in Harness." He loved his work, and was loyal to a fault to Honeywell, always at the ready to satisfy its demands whatever those demands might be. Not surprisingly, he considered my speech a personal betrayal.

The United States in the 1980s experienced an artificial economic boom (e.g., Reagan "Star War" years) against a plethora of scandals (e.g., Savings & Loan Institutions), while American corporate management never stumbled upon a fad it didn't love as long as it was simple, inexpensive and didn't disturb its power. In my experience, "Participative Management" was consistent with that mindset.

Panic was in the air, which I came to call, The Prison of Panic called "Now"!

America's hard goods markets at home and abroad were fast disappearing, while, paradoxically, the American workforce had seemingly changed overnight to a professional class of workers, only management still treated them as if nothing had changed.

During these years of panic, rather than step back, pause, take inventory and study the changing tide of events, it was "do anything, everything now!"

The speech which follows was given in that climate.

For my punishment, I was placed on the equivalent of "house arrest," banned from writing papers or giving speeches for 18-months. But by something akin to serendipity, I emerged from this to be promoted in 1986 to Honeywell Europe's management team in its Brussels, Belgium headquarters.

There I saw first-hand that corporate Europe was as messed up as corporate America. Honeywell's European national franchises had retrogressed to operating essentially as feudal fiefdoms after WWII with the managing directors as lords and masters of all that they surveyed.

As passive and hierarchically inert as were American workers, European workers, country to country, were even more so. It was a perfect situation for an OD study, which I quickly launched into with the idea of a subsequent book in mind (see Work Without Managers, 1991, 2nd edition, 2014).

As Director of Human Resources Planning & Development, an OD position, it was soon apparent, however, that my new boss in Brussels had no idea what OD was or what it could do.

Whereas in the States I had been given carte blanche to practice OD, he saw my role as that of a traditional technocrat with management, not the entire organization as my OD client, failing to understand that OD assesses equally the efficacy of management as it does that of the workforce. This conflict in perspective didn't make for a happy marriage. His persona appears in the next segment as the *"Winning Side Saddler,"* or the constant pleaser but with a hidden agenda as opposed to *"Happily in Harness"* of my boss in the States who had no agenda at all other than that of satisfying his Honeywell superiors.

So, in a not too subtle way, going against the grain expresses an intellectual perspective that the reader will find in this 1984 speech and subsequently conveyed thematically in my other books and articles in this genre.

The germ of ideas that leads to books is active in the subconscious mind as a working life unfolds and is therefore basically a recording of that fact.

GOING AGAINST THE GRAIN!

"Time is painted with a lock before, and bald behind, signing thereby that we must take time by the forelock, for when it is once passed there is no recalling it."

—**Jonathan Swift,**
Anglo-Irish satirist, essayist and poet

SOMETIMES IT IS necessary to step out of the shadows and take a stand, not because it is a courageous act, but because it is necessary. Martine Luther did it early in the 16th century, many others have done it along the way. Some are as modest as this one, all involve personal and professional risk.

A CAREER CHANGING KEYNOTE SPEECH

This speech was given on March 30, 1984 at the Caribbean Gulf Resort Hotel, Clearwater, Florida, to a Conference of Department of Contract Administration Services (DCAS), which included an audience of some 200 government officials, senior military officers of U.S. Army, Navy, Air Force and Marines, and consultants, as well as Honeywell Avionics' CEO and senior managers. At the time, I was an organizational development psychologist for Honeywell's Clearwater, Florida facility, the host of the conference.

This conference convened during the collective hysteria of the time. Japan and South East Asia had quietly captured a significant portion of pristine American manufacturing markets. In 1980, Tom Brokaw of NBC television, bringing attention to this fact, presented an hour-long tutorial, *"Japan Can, Why Can't We?"*

Japan, Inc.'s growing dominance in manufacturing, included the automotive industry, machine tools, electronics, home appliances, light fixtures, and steel production. Human Resources (HR) stepped into the breach with Quality Control Circles (QCC), teaming, employee empowerment and participative management, not as a carefully framed design of the problem, but in an attempt to replicate the Japanese miracle.

One of my functions was to direct the QCC Program, which at the time, was one of the largest in the country. Honeywell +Avionics was a facility of 4,000 with 80 percent professionals or white collar workers and 20 percent blue-collar. Among the professionals were 1,000 engineers many with advanced degrees in their respective disciplines. Blue-collar workers responded to quality circles, professionals did not.

Little note was made of the fact that Japan was a *group oriented culture* versus America's *individual oriented society*. Nor did many stop to consider that 80 percent of Japanese workers were blue-collar whereas 20 percent of ours were. NBC pricked the nation's denial button flooding its conscience with collective hysteria.

From my perspective in the trenches, this was a charade. Workers had little power and less participation beyond cosmetic change, which had little bearing on performance or outcomes. Even blue-collar workers with the best of intentions were essentially treading water and going nowhere. I felt it was time to speak out, and go against the grain. To Honeywell's credit, no limitation was put on what I might say.

PARTICIPATIVE MANAGEMENT AN ADVERSARY POINT OF VIEW

INTRODUCTION

Man is a pragmatic animal. He does what he does because he thinks it is the best way to do it. He may listen to a contrary way of doing it. If his heart is not in it, there is little chance he'll give his best.

During the past several years, I have attempted to facilitate the shift from paternalistic to participative management, from centrally located decision-making to autonomous work groups. This work was conducted in an ideal environment here at Honeywell.

For one, the team concept had been employed among the hourly workforce since 1972. For another, all of the operations of this 4,000-employee facility were on one beautiful campus in the Florida Sunbelt. For yet another, management had been educated in Quality Control Circle concepts with countless organizational development (OD) interventions, resulting in a significant number of changes. These were however essentially cosmetic changes: e.g., changing the lighting in workstations, having more flexibility in dress code, providing longer breaks, changing work hours, and so on.

In any case, this facility has perhaps the longest sustained participative working climate in the continental United States. There are 110 Quality Circle teams with more than 1,000 members of the workforce participating in the process. Additionally, there is a pilot program of some 200 professional workers and their managers immersed in "Shared Management," which is touted as a "step beyond Quality Circles."

Virtually everything management could reasonably be expected to do has been done for the workforce. Are workers happy? Reasonably so. Are they productive? Relatively speaking, yes. Are they doing as much as they are capable of doing? No. Do they have the entrepreneur spirit? Not on a bet.

Then are you saying all this has been for naught? Compliance is not cooperation, and this is compliance. Fear or coercion is the motivator. Workers are aware of *The Great Depression* in the Steel and Automotive Industries, and say, "There go I but for the grace of my employer."

Meanwhile, management has been in a long slump, thinking in terms of 1955 competition and been close to panic. It has resulted in turning OD from a hybrid of psychology, industrial engineering, and sociology into a burgeoning profession without portfolio. Undaunted by this fact management has stopped everything to listen to what we have to say.

"Process" has become the magic word, along with "systemic problems," in other words, explanatory rather than operational approaches. Jargon gets the attention of most managers. The irony is that this shock wave that has gone through management has escaped the attention of the workforce. They are huddled in passivity willing to do whatever without complaint.

PARTICIPATIVE MANAGEMENT'S HIDDEN AGENDAS

Paternalistic management was authoritative, task oriented and bottom line driven. Conversely, the workforce was management dependent, authoritatively compliant, selfishly motivated and bottom line indifferent. *Enter the sobriquet, "Participative Management."*

This implies that management is people centered and process conscious with the workforce expected to be cooperative and motivated. No surprise the workforce for this renewed attention felt good about itself and its workplace — even happy — but still bottom line disinterested. The good intentions did not translate into an entrepreneur spirit or productive work.

A recent experience illustrates my point. I was talking to a production line supervisor, who thinks these changes are terrific. I asked him about a colleague. "Have you seen him lately?" I asked

"Oh, yeah. Over the weekend."

"How are things going in his operation?" I continued.

"I don't know," he replied. "We didn't talk about the company business. We talked about the new businesses we're starting."

After he told me a bit more about this, I offered, "I guess it's the American spirit to be in business for yourself."
"Yeah," he smiled. "You could say that, you want to be independent. Be your own boss. Have something of your own."

Here was a supervisor who could see through cosmetic changes without knowing he was doing so, and was keeping his options open if things didn't work out. Imagine the mindset of the people working for him.

THE RISE OF THE NON-DOER DOERS

The organization is made up of those that manage and those that do. Those that manage have grown into a force unto themselves with layer on layer of middle management created to move the paperwork while acting as a buttress between the feudal lords of industry and the masses.

Next there has been created parallel organizations, which support and serve management, but who neither manage nor do (I belong to this exalted community). These non-doer doers have been called "professionals," the white-collar class and "staff" to "line" (i.e., to the doers). You find these workers in personnel, finance, security, maintenance, marketing, and even engineering. Once a need is created for their services, it is impossible to imagine being without that service or them.

Since WWII, pyramid building has become something of a natural phenomenon in all professions. Translated, the organization has too many people doing too many non-thing things. So, the first problem that should have been noted when our competitive edge was slipping was this organizational excess baggage, that is, one manager to every ten-twelve workers (industrial average) and one staff employee per every four managers (industrial average). Scaling down this pyramid, alone, amounts to megabucks in savings not to mention a much sprier and leaner organization. So, what have we done? Where has the focus been? On the doers, of course. The powerful on the powerless. In transactional terms, the Parent on the Child.

Since the ownership spirit is precisely what we are trying to instill and since the referenced supervisor had been sent to a considerable number of courses and laboratories to develop his consciousness concerning such ownership, I said, "How does this differ from what you are doing here?"

He looked at me in amazement. "I don't want to do this all my life." Sensing that I wanted to know more, he continued.

"My wife is my partner in this." He started to laugh. "She has a real problem paying the help $4.00 an hour."

"Joe, that's not even a living wage," I responded. His expression was defiant — "So?"

This intrigued me. "As you know from your own people," I continued, "They want more money not because they have done more, but because they need more. It seems you are faced with the same problem in your private enterprise that we are facing here."

He scratched his head. "I never thought of it like that."

"No, possibly not," I offered. "Perhaps because it is coming out of your own pocket now and you can feel the pinch."

"Yeah. I see what you mean," he replied.

And this was an experienced supervisor who had been given all the training and tools, which were designed to create a feeling of ownership, but he, too, was bottom line disinterested.

ENTER INTERNATIONAL ASSOCIATION OF QUALITY CIRCLES (IAQC)

A whole organization has sprung into being, IAQC, with a strategy to get the "most out of the least" — and they have. Dr. J. M. Juran calls this the problem solving strategy of the "trivial many." Juran and others point out, given the scope of what quality circles encompass, if doers knock out all the fat and become lean as a tooth, they still have solved only 15 percent of the problems facing the organization.

Meanwhile, management, which has become too much and too many has difficulty turning the microscope on itself for fear it will see the "big C" — Capital neglect—for not having dealt purposefully with the critical 85 percent.

Management has purposely established a caste and class system of non-doers who are confused. Just as doers are inclined to be bottom line disinterested, they are more inclined to mistake self-interested outcomes (department goals) as bottom line, which could be even worse.

THE ANSWER TO BOTTOM LINE: DISINTEREST, OR SERIAL/ PARALLEL CAREERS

Add to this the fact that in this changing work climate where all sorts of wonderful programs are being sponsored, the workforce sees its benefits shrinking, its pay frozen, its promotional opportunities disappearing and its job security eroding. Is it any wonder that workers and managers go out and start businesses on the side?

I was writing this in the cafeteria the other day and there in the booth next to me was a company staff engineer selling an insurance policy to an administrative worker — two non-doers doing personal business on company time without apology, guilt or concern. It was as if "I have the right. I get this opportunity in lieu of pay...," or whatever.

For comparative purposes, out of this population of 4,000, there are 800 production workers (20%), 1,000 engineers (25%), 400 managers (10%), and 1,800 other professionals (45%). No less than one quarter of these professional workers are believed to have serial or parallel careers, much of which is conducted on company time. From selling real estate to selling diamonds, from pet fish to insurance, from restaurant to management consulting, from private teaching to private investigating, from motel operations to hardware store managing.

What all this seems to indicate is that a great number of attractive solutions have been developed without a clear understanding of what the problem is. Meanwhile, the rank and file are oblivious to the anguish and pain common to the organization. They fail to care because they don't see it as their problem. Let the "organization" solve it. They see the organization as distinct from them, as if it has life without their blood in it. If the organization bleeds, they would be hard pressed to see themselves bleeding with it, that is, until the organization goes out of business or moves elsewhere.

To understand how this dilemma has evolved one must revisit the history of the complex organization.

THE SEEDS OF THE PROBLEM

Two hundred years ago, when most of the business of business was conducted in small guilds, there was great informality. People did what they did best. Somebody was in charge but it was an additional role besides being a line contributor. There were no job descriptions, no performance appraisals, no reward and recognition programs, no staff support, nobody else to blame if a product did not sell because it was made poorly or overpriced. Survival was predicated on doing the best you were able to do with the skills you had, the materials and tools you had to work with, and pride and sense of ownership you brought to the work. Work was love made visible.

People knew who they were by what they did. Often, the work was dirty, grimy, exhausting with little profit, hardly a living wage. We romanticize this period now, but in reality, it was a harsh, hard existence. The guild workers had to work long hours, seventy hours a week was not uncommon. There were few if any entitlements, only work.

Were they happy? Not particularly. Were they productive? Extremely so. Were they doing as much as they were capable? Generally speaking, yes. Did they have the entrepreneur spirit? In buckets! They had no choice. The wolf was always gaining ground on them.

Then the *Industrial Revolution* exploded into their midst. These self-directed, self-managed, self-motivated workers were forced by necessity into a strange environment of huge machines and masses of people.

There was no model that fit the purposes of the complex organization. The closest model was the bureaucratic structure of the Roman Catholic Church and the National Army. The goal of the church was to save your soul; the goal of the army was to save your life. No confusion there. Everyone knew, understood, and could relate to those common goals.

But the complex organization was an organization of sub-organizations and sub-sub-organizations, all with their own goals along with every individual's hidden agenda. Meanwhile, workers, who were never comfortable with all these goals, dreamed in terms of their own private agenda. They saw themselves as renting their bodies for a price, leaving their minds safely at home, which included their motivation. They saw the factory as a voluntary prison that they entered because they had no other choice. They couldn't compete with the factory from the guild, nor from the farm. They had given up their freedom out of economic necessity, the fear of survival.

And so, from the opening chapters of the *Industrial Revolution* to the *Post-Industrial Age,* the worker has never identified with the factory as "his" factory, or as an extension of his will and dreams.

This has been the domain of only a precious few, the senior managers of the organization. This is where the power rests, not in the stockholders nor, indeed, in capitalistic society. Curiously, senior management operates very similarly to the management of the guilds. There is a *common will* dedicated to the same set of principles and a consensus bottom line. It is arguably, senior managers' organization and their hide if it falls on hard times.

More curious still, the doers and the senior managers are cut from the same atavistic cloth. They both speak the language of the guilds. What makes for the problem of the modern organization is that there are ten or twelve layers of bodies between senior management and these doers.

What these doers hear, then, is a language that is remote and beyond their interests and comprehension. Instead, what they hear are demands, threats, and candy-coated enticements, directives that a child hears from a concerned or frustrated parent. And appropriately, like a child, the expected behavior follows:

- Testing the firmness of the demand.
- Accepting punishment as justification for challenging the demands.
- Learning to say the right words while continuing to misbehave.
- Treating the machines (as toys) with disdain, neglect and contempt.
- Seeing the organization as blocking them from what they want to do.
- Crying, whining and embarrassing the organization into submitting to its will.
- Feeling angry and hostile and unfulfilled after getting its own way.
- Telling the organization what it wants to hear rather than what it needs to know.
- Behaving in a way that says, "I want more" — when more is given — "I still want more" — "I will always want more."

The workforce is frozen in the adolescent-infantile state notwithstanding all the programs and slogans, which would suggest otherwise. Put another way, the modern organization gets very little real productivity out of its people — perhaps only about 30 percent of what they could do.

Does this mean most workers don't care? Of course not. It means that the structure of the organization does not fit the tasks — the structure should enhance the accomplishment of the tasks, which too often it does not.

More importantly, workers are not treated as adults, as full partners in the enterprise. Oh! The words are used, but management's behavior does not compute with the words.

Granted, a great deal of attention is being given the environment in terms of Quality Circles, Quality of Work Life, and Quality of Work. There are also cross-cultural awareness programs designed to get this blueprint on to the factory floor. Management styles are being modified in quest of the magic formula that will make the organization more productive.

What have these activities achieved? At best, marginal if ephemeral results. Why? The majority still march to the programmed cadence of terminal adolescence that has been the organization's drumbeat for decades. Why should anyone be surprised for workers' inability to respond with maturity?

MARRIED TO MACHINE AGE THINKING - ERIK ERIKSON'S MODEL OF HUMAN DEVELOPMENT

"The reasonable man adapts himself to the world, the unreasonable one persists in trying to adapt the world to himself Therefore, all progress depends on the unreasonable man."

—**George Bernard Shaw,** Maxims *for Revolution* (1903)

Labor unions are in sharp decline, while management's union, Human Resources (HR) is soaring with its cosmetic interventions.

Workers feel betrayed by labor unions as management's adversary, and exploited by HR as management's advocate. The "best and brightest" have become cynical and turned to making money rather than making a difference. That legacy has contributed to the economic crisis.

The uncoupling of workers from managers has widened as managers no longer lead and workers no longer follow. Surprisingly, we have survived despite management's insensitivity and workers' immaturity during the *Machine Age*.

To understand this, let us walk through a cultural no man's land guided by Erik Erikson's six styles of human personality development: (1) autonomy; (2) trust; (3) initiative; (4) accomplishment; (5) identity; and (6) intimacy.

Erikson's model supports the premise that management is dealing with a wrongly conditioned workforce for the times, a workforce that enjoys little autonomy, only contrived trust, little opportunity to take the initiative or to sense personal accomplishment, which leads to a crisis in identity and an inability to demonstrate intimacy.

The workforce experiences from the crib to the company a high need to please which marks its arrested development. When workers as adults are needed, they are nowhere to be found.

It was surreal but nonetheless true when management thought it could construct arbitrary systems, such as Quality Circles and empowerment programs such as *Participative Management* and workers would respond with maturity and satisfaction. Obviously, this has not been the case.

Instead, the new wave of challenges and opportunities have been met with confusion if not shame, mistrust, guilt, a sense of insecurity, and isolation. This has perplexed management as it has failed to see how more than fifty years of co-dependency has resulted in a workforce essentially mired in terminal adolescence.

What needs to be done, fortunately, is revealed in Erikson's model. Management needs to maintain patience with the process. It needs to cut back on its demands, and look for ways to cultivate workers for the long haul. This can be done by encouraging workers to do the right things rather than everything right. Workers know what makes the difference. Management needs only to solicit their views on common problems, which will gradually turn workers around from passive to active responders.

If this sounds like making workers full partners in the process, we are on the same page. Reality, when it is positive and reinforcing, finds workers at the ready, but when reality is negative and demanding it is another story. It will not be easy for workers to become more responsive and responsible. If they do, the dividends are considerable:

- A sense of autonomy will build self-control, which will lead to self-management demonstrating the willpower of disciplined behavior;
- A sense of trust will fuel the drive and motivation to have faith in the future;
- A sense of initiative will give self-direction and purpose to work;

- A sense of accomplishment will lead to competence;
- A sense of identity will lead to loyalty and fidelity;
- A sense of intimacy will promote affiliation and love;
- Personality development involves the formation of trust.

Trust is obviously an issue in most organizations and only slightly above the "dog eat dog" level. A sense of *autonomy* is constantly denied until most adults are products of learned helplessness with a high need to please others without any idea how to please themselves.

The sense of *accomplishment* is also thwarted because expediency dictates there is a right way, which is translated the only way. This leaves little room for *initiative* or for failure, which is the learning phase. In the absence of initiative and accomplishment, there is little room for personal satisfaction.

Identity is a stage that most would admit not handling too well. Confusion between self-demands and role demands leads to *identity crises*.

When so handicapped, workers become other directed with little idea what makes them tick other than being dependent on their bosses for direction, or counter dependent on the workplace for their total well-being.

The psychological shrinking of America has created an industry for mid-life identity crises. One in every three Americans seeks psychotherapy or counseling from a psychiatrist, psychologist, physician, psychotherapist, guidance counselor, preacher, teacher, guru or friend.

Yet perhaps the hardest is to attain a *sense of intimacy*. Sex is not intimacy. Love is. Sex and love can merge into intimacy but the problem is not only intimacy with others but with ourselves.

We are interested in having good friends, but the most important friendship must be with ourselves. If we cannot be intimate with ourselves, then intimacy with others in a sham.

THE SEARCH FOR A QUICK CURE

The modern worker is a new entity. He is more skilled, better educated and self-confident. He also has different values, beliefs and expectations as well as interests. He doesn't respond well to blarney.

He has power in his knowledge and is self-motivated and the new kid on the block. When he comes into an organization, it is like hitting a wall when he is expected to be management dependent or counter dependent on the company for his or her total well-being.

He is not timid, insecure, unskilled, undereducated, and naive, but it is soon clear to him that he is expected to take orders, be polite, obedient, punctual, and passive and appreciate being taken care of

When he is unresponsive to charismatic leadership, and doesn't see the company as "his family," and fails to follow company policies and procedures to the letter he finds himself in the wrong place at the wrong time. The irony is that he may just be what the company needs.

This has been the dilemma. Professionally trained workers find themselves being treated as if blue-collar workers when they see themselves as decision-makers and not passive responders.

Rather than admit the workforce is dominated by this new worker with fully eight out of ten, and soon nine out of ten workers being of such a mindset and temperament, companies have attempted to make them fit. Many pundits and writers have been at the ready to oblige management.

Terrence Deal and Allan Kennedy in *"Corporate Culture"* see the problem in terms of knowing what the company stands for; Bob Waterman and Tom Peters in *"Search for Excellence"* claim the best bet is to copy successful companies; and John Nesbit in *"Megatrends "sees* visions beyond the pale of the cockeyed optimist.

These prescriptions fail to deal with Erikson's six stages which can flourish only in a culture that supports them.

ELEVEN CORPORATE HABITS IN THE WAY

The Problem with Top-Down Communications.

Operationally, strategic planning doesn't necessarily translate into tactical communications. What is proposed in the Boardroom is compromised with too many filters to pass through to the operations level. Consequently, internal stress and accelerating external demands mount to the point that problems go unreported or are misconstrued and timely decisions are not made.

Management by Objectives (MBOs) in practice, has proven counterproductive, time consuming, expensive and ineffective.

Compartmentalizing objectives, and then rewarding each department for accomplishing its objectives has proven illusory as systems analyst Russell Ackoff has shown:

> *If you take a system apart to identify its components, and then operate those components as well as possible, the system as a whole will not behave as well as it could. It is counterintuitive to Machine Age thinking, but nonetheless true, if you have a system that is behaving as well as it could, then none of its parts will be.*

Nonconfrontational Style of Management

Tension and conflict are normal fare in an organization. Asking questions, or disputing the problem solving strategy are necessary to have a vibrant, engaged and energetic work climate. Harmony is the antithesis of efficacy as *managed conflict* is the glue that holds an operation on task. Americans tend to protest infrequently but violently instead of frequently and politely. It is not necessary that everyone like each other for an operation to be successful, but it is important that everyone respect and esteem each other's contribution.

Management manages the way it is paid.

When lip service is given to quality, it is understood that compensation and promotion depend upon meeting schedule at any cost. Corners are cut, and ethical standards compromised to meet the bottom line. Workers see this and become cynical.

Management has outsourced Personnel Management to Human Resources with dire consequences.

Feeling international competition, decaying infrastructure of plants and equipment, and especially obsolescent manpower technical skills, and demotivated workers, management turned to human resources to solve its problems. The result has been a series of cosmetic interventions that have made the workplace like a playground at the expense of performance.

Management is obsessed with order making it vulnerable to chaos and disorder.

In the *Machine Age*, when everything was in its place and there was a place for everything, this made sense. Work, workers and the workplace were like a well-oiled machine with predictable outcomes and little variance, as it was essentially a robotic environment with workers behaving like interchangeable parts. That has all changed in the era of the professional worker, except in the workplace.

The company in attempting to be all things to its people has ended in being a disappointment to everyone.

When things were going smoothly and profits were soaring, management flirted with lifetime employment, and entitlement programs that had little to do with performance. Now when markets are shrinking, and costs are soaring, management plays the heavy. US Steel and Alcoa learned this the hard way. A program was initiated in the 1960s in which every five years veteran employees would be given an additional 13-weeks paid furlough.

The objective was to leverage employees to greater productivity Instead of traveling or honing their skills, most workers got second jobs. When back to work at US Steel and Alcoa, now enjoying the income from two jobs, many attempted to work both jobs, which diminished performance, and led instead to anger with management.

The John Wayne "Lone Ranger" Mindset

Some company brass take pride in going it alone, taking big risks, cutting out new territory with a flamboyance that nothing untoward can touch them, until it does sending the company into an economic tailspin with workers in the end to pay. These no nonsense cowboys of reckless enterprise led to the Savings & Loan scandal where the books were cooked and people went to prison.

The Problem of Professionalism

Professionalism has evolved as we have moved through the post-industrial to modernity and into postmodernity all within a generation or so. We have become an acquisitive society not only in materialism but also in terms of credentials. We measure capability by those who have degrees, and give little consideration to those who do not, as if a degree holder has a right to a job simply for being credentialed. Intelligence is what intelligence does, not a BS or BA designation. Credentials are not a shorthand for competence. Typically, when a professional runs into career stagnation, he goes back to school to get an MBA or Ph.D.

The Confusion between Tasks and Structures

No one is likely to argue that the norms for one company would apply equally to another. There are discrete cultures to every company. When the lights are dimmed at 6 p.m., it tells workers it is time to go home. If there are staff meetings routinely every morning, it means work is secondary to your expected presence. If you want to stay after six, the dimming of the lights tells you it can wait until tomorrow. If you prefer to work alone but everything is done in teams, then it is in team meetings where you should be. If none of this appeals to you, then it is best that you move on, but most people don't.

> *The structure of work determines the function of work; the function of work creates the workplace culture; the workplace culture dictates organizational behavior; and that behavior if it is consistent with your drives will be enhancing; if it is not*

you are in the wrong place.

What does it mean for the company? It means some companies will soar, some will vegetate, and others will flounder and expire. It depends on how much the structure supports the tasks at hand.

Human Resources has unwittingly become Management's Union.

Management is remarkably dependent on a buffer between it and its people. Be that buffer an adversary or advocate is immaterial, the function is basically the same. Moreover, just as the labor union movement grew out of an erosion of worker power in the industrial organization, the Human Resources movement has grown out of an erosion of management power in the complex organization. Labor unions and human resources have had a similar function: insuring organizational survival. The reason for drawing special attention to this "new unionism" is that it reveals, once again, how precariously the organization is in transition. Also, it indicates the void between the workforce and management is growing wider.

With the labor unions, you may recall, union leaders bought into management's emphasis on productivity. Their attention was diverted from the erosion of worker power or control of what they did to sacrificing this for entitlements, compensation and job security. Now that has also eroded. Labor unions were willing to give management increasing control as long as management made pay and entitlement concessions. This has hurt workers and management alike. Management believed that paying workers more would motivate them to do more. One need look no further than the steel and automotive industries to see that this did not work.

Now, we have the "New Union," Human Resources, orchestrating interventions that have turned the workplace into a playground. Just as management gave the labor unions the money they said they needed, management is now giving Human Resources the power to promote morale with cosmetic perks:

(1) From designated parking to work concessions;

(2) From touchy-feely supervision to extraordinary fringe benefits;

(3) From beautiful work areas to wonderful group programs.

Whereas the labor union got management and the worker to think in terms of money concessions, Human Resources has gotten management and the worker to think in terms of comfort and climatic luxury. The net result has been in both cases a demotivated workforce vacillating between comfort and complacency. It is time management becomes less dependent on advocacy (Human Resources) or adversarial (Labor Unions) relationships, and more on workers and management becoming truly partners in enterprise.

And So Where Do We Go From Here?

What I have attempted to do here is admittedly a risky analysis of a complex problem. There is no way such an analysis can be made without stepping on some toes including the hand that feeds me. Be that as it may, I have been waiting for someone to surface these realities:

That the modern complex organization is out of balance and has got to regain that balance;

That balance cannot be discovered by ignoring history or by embracing untested new ideas;

That workers conduct themselves the way they have been programmed to work, and that conditioning cannot be summarily rejected by instituting prosthetic corrections (re: Quality Circles and Participative Management Programs);

That management has had a haughty dependence on technology (or things), and a horrifying disregard and ignorance of workers (as persons);

That workers have a fundamental need to contribute and own what they do because work provides pride and identity;

That workers need to experience growth in order to feel worthwhile;

That workers will behave as children when treated like children;

That the organization in the modern era has become increasingly immature in the home, church, school, and community as well as in the workplace;

That immaturity is a product of believing what is best for the individual without knowing what the individual needs, values, believes or expects.

That *Participative Management* doesn't have a ghost of a chance until the gap is closed between the adolescent and the adult mindset in the workplace;

That *Participative Management* is a ruse if there is actually no shift in organizational power.

    Having said all this, I think a first step is to recognize that the "management of things" and the "management of people" are discretely different functions; that managers and consultants must realize that listening is more powerful than telling; that framing the problem is more important than generating solutions; that we are on the threshold of a wonderful tomorrow if we can "let go" of our faulty premises and precious assumptions and let a little reality guide the way which includes recognizing and an exploiting the advantage of *The Ascent of the Working Woman*, which is proving quite a mountain to climb as the *Feminine Paradigm* and *Masculine Paradigm* are still not operating on the same circuit.

LEADERSHIP MANIFESTO FOR THE TWENTY-FIRST CENTURY

"The wise man has his follies no less than the fool; but herein lies the difference — the follies of the fool are known to the world, but are hidden from himself; the follies of the wise man are known to himself, but hidden from the world"
—**Caleb C. Colton** (1780-1832) English clergyman

Leadership is in a state of retreat bordering on confusion. Not only is leadership out-of-date but out-of-touch with the reality of work and workers. Leadership models are now in jeopardy because they were designed for another time and another workforce. Institutions today go from crisis to crisis, scandal to scandal, outrage to outrage. We wait for the other shoe to drop and have become the United States of Anxiety.

—**James R. Fisher, Jr.**, *Misdirected Leadership Ideals*

The Chronic Problem: Typology of Leaderless Leadership

VENERATED former CEO of General Electric (GE), Jack Welch, never realized how short he was until he saw a picture of his high school sports team. Welch became the ultimate workaholic to compensate for this. One day he found himself "like a man standing 6 feet 4 with a full head of hair," and the quintessential executive and corporate leader of America.[1] Welch had his GE management team and rank and file basking in his reflected glory with soaring accomplishments.

John Francis "Jack" Welch, Jr. was born November 9, 1935 of Irish American parents, his father a Boston & Maine Railroad conductor, his mother, a homemaker. He has been focused, industrious and successful throughout his life.

During high school, he worked summers as a golf caddy, newspaper delivery boy, shoe salesman, and drill press operator.

At Salem High School, although small, he participated in baseball, football, and captained the hockey team.

Late in his senior year, he was accepted at the University of Massachusetts Amherst, where he studied chemical engineering, and worked summers in chemical engineering at Sunoco and PPG Industries, graduating in 1957 with a Bachelor of Science degree in chemical engineering.

He turned down several corporate offers in order to attend graduate school at the University of Illinois where he earned a Master's degree in 1960 and a PhD in chemical engineering the following year.

A score of years later, he became chairman and CEO of General Electric and held that position from 1981 to 2001.

During his tenure at GE, the company's value rose 4,000 percent. In 2006, his net worth was estimated at $720 million.

When he retired from GE, he took a severance payment of $417 million, the largest such payment at the time in history.

Despite this impressive portfolio and record of success, he has had his critics.

Academics, such as Rahesh Khurana of Harvard, are not so easily impressed. Dr. Khurana suggests that leadership at GE has been superb for the past 100 years and that Welch's contribution to that leadership is consistent with that reputation. The system, Khurana points out, created the climate for such leadership to evolve. The system created Jack Welch, he did not create the system.[2]

Being newsworthy these days is not a function of culture or inconspicuous performance, but personality and charismatic appeal, where the mystique of the brash 14-year-old mindset in the 60-year-old bodysuit becomes the prototype of what constitutes leadership.

Welch fits the mold and worked to create the impression he was a regular guy and working stiff, which he was even if he made 700 times more than the typical worker. What role did the 300,000 GE employees play in this success? Qualitatively, they contributed a great deal, but not necessarily quantitatively in terms of compensation. This, of course, is not exclusively CEO Welch's fault, as he is as much a product of the system as are these workers.

Why should a single CEO at the top of an organization be treated like royalty? This makes no sense when we consider that thriving organizations assign decisions to workers who are close to the level of consequences and depend on timely feedback from these workers to generate strategies with positive outcomes.

Yet MBA students are taught to focus on the management of things with only passing attention to the leadership of people as persons. They learn that people are expendable and are necessary only to accomplish given goals; the less people the better the financial advantage. One executive took this philosophy to heart and instituted a 20-40-60 plan: *re-evaluate all employees who have* *had 20 years of service, who are more than 40 years of age, and/or earn $60,000 or more.*

Senior managers at K-Mart sued the company in the US Court of Appeals (February 14, 1995) for this alleged practice. This case against K-Mart proved not to contain probative evidence as it was an oral rather than a written policy. K-Mart filed for bankruptcy protection in 2002. Ex-CEO Charles Conaway was ordered to pay $10 million, reduced to $5.5 million for misleading shareholders about the retailer's prospects before its 2002 bankruptcy.

What is most disturbing about this case is that once trust is broken struggle for survival is doubly difficult, as is the case with K-Mart today. The careers of corporate sinners, however, go on as they remain essentially unscathed. Charles Conaway was fired from K-Mart for hiding the company's credit status from stockholders, only to become COO of CVS Pharmacy.'

These outrages display the arrogance of power, and represent a corporate society adrift without a rudder. They show the love of total war. Competition must be obliterated not simply beaten. The enemy must be destroyed, no mercy granted. If these actions cause collateral damage, such as people losing their jobs, so be it. This is manifestly *leaderless leadership,* and reflects the dilemma of leadership today.

Leadership discussions assume everyone is talking about the same thing. Leadership often is personified in a charismatic leader (President Kennedy), a central figure (Pope John Paul II), or a person in the organization (Jack Welch).

Leadership invariably is reduced to an individual at the helm. I find this too narrow a perspective. I don't think charisma is relevant, and I don't believe leadership is personified in a central figure. I believe leadership is organic, an all-encompassing phenomenon in which everyone is a leader or no one is!

Typology of Leadership Behavior

Our institutions are failing and such failures are always human. The fact that scandals grow nastier is evidence only that we have a problem — not a morality issue but a contextual problem. Because the leadership culture programs the way workers behave, corporations get the leadership and behavior they deserve. Crisis, scandal and outrage do not occur in a vacuum. They are unwitting products of corporate design, and when the design is wrong, the social termites or "six silent killers" produce their silent havoc.[4]

Circumstances are forcing a re-evaluation of leadership. More than a decade ago, I suggested that work could be conducted more efficiently without managers, that performance appraisals were a costly and counterproductive travesty, and that the total quality movement was an expediency driven by crisis management.' Time has not changed my mind.

People are failing, and we need a typology to describe the humanness of this failure. After observing people for over four decades, I have gleaned the typology of leadership behaviors described in the following segment. If you notice that these types focus on failure, it is because I have encountered far more failures than successes.

Manipulators

Manipulators believe everyone has his or her price, and the leadership system was made for exploitation. The more able the exploiter, the faster this *leaderless leader* rises to a position of consequence. Manipulators conceal hidden agendas and naked ambition, deceptively promoting an image of being straight arrows. Their weapons are fear and intimidation; first they try and cajole others to accept their perspective and, if that doesn't work, they threaten.

Frustrated Participants

These *leaderless leaders* believe in the corporate system and see themselves as dedicated managers. They often are frustrated but are reluctant to complain. When they find inconsistencies in company policy, flagrant violations of fairness issues, etc., they feel their role is to protect the company's image without protest. After a particularly exasperating experience, one frustrated participants was asked what he would do. He replied, "What I always do. Suck it up and move on."

Inside Outsider

Some *leaderless leaders* possess critical specialist skills, often having professional credentials that rank with officers of the company. Although they arrive to enhance their status by impressing others with their unique skills, they don't attain the authority exercised by generalists and are never considered key players. They experience the paradox of being needed but not wanted. To the old guard they are cowboys, to the new guard, necessary evils.

Winning Side Saddlers

This type of *leaderless leader* appears more frequently at higher levels of the organization. They are consummate pleasers, which endears them to their bosses. They focus on what is wanted, not what is needed. They are chameleons with the capacity to change camouflage at a moment's notice. Should a power shift be eminent, they are the first to leave the old saddle and climb into the stirrups of the new boss.

Nostalgic Elitists

Remnants of a less egalitarian past, these *leaderless leaders* long for the way it once was, when a clear demarcation existed between workers and managers. Today's less structured, open-systems approach causes them great pain. They cannot fathom why their authority is challenged, why the less gifted are treated as equals, or why their superiority is no longer self-evident. Nostalgic elitists see a more permissive culture emerging, where everybody does his or her own thing. They fail to recognize that creativity and chaos are related and that open systems spawn creativity. Their attitude alienates peers, frustrates subordinates, and agonizes superiors.

Waiters in the Wings

These pragmatic *leaderless leaders* marshal resources, plan strategies, and develop tactics. They periodically compare their careers to company progress, having no desire to tie their future to a sinking ship. Their ambition is not obvious because they feel no need to campaign openly. Although they seem relaxed, they usually are impatient and are not willing to wait very long for recognition and promotion. Operationally, they make themselves indispensable and are self-confident, but they are not cheerleaders. They are balanced and maintain perspective without being easily ruffled. This makes them calming influences in crises, and inadvertently threatening to those who are less secure.

Happily in Harness

These contented *leaderless leaders* love what they do and are appreciative and generous, good co-workers and supervisors, competent without being arrogant. They create a climate for peers and subordinates to grow — even if they are not always effective coaches. They are trusted and fair, consistent and honest. They never think of countermanding an executive order or bad mouthing a superior. They take pride in their ability to do the job, but are surprisingly tolerant of those who don't. Although laziness is foreign to them, they remain philosophical about lazy people. They are unlikely to rock the boat.

Quiet Soldiers

Although these *leaderless leaders* may appear similar to those that are happily in harness, they differ in some striking ways. They are comfortable as followers and identify with subordinates but are not necessarily content in their jobs. They do only what they are told and don't take risks. They have talent but little resolve. They are apt to accept untenable situations rather than complain. "Not my job," echoes in their silence. Simply put, they are passive passengers on their own ship of destiny. In the past, quiet soldiers were the impetus to paternalistic authority, but now they are more often part of the logjam. They are an atavistic holdover from an anachronistic system.

Victims

This martyr-like *leaderless leadership* pattern is displayed by managers who expect to be trusted without being trustworthy, given cherished assignments without being dependable, and taken at their word without being reliable. They delight in the failures of others, but find no humor when others delight in theirs. When others fail, it is because they're incompetent, when they fail, it's because others let them down. "If only" is their litany and mantra.

Unbending Idealists

Idealizing life and living in a dream world, these *leaderless leaders* see themselves as saviors of lost causes and lost souls, explaining away failures. "He didn't mean to steal the laptop. He just forgot to bring it back." As apologists, they envision a world where there is no conflict or contradiction, only utopian harmony. The problem is that managed conflict is the adhesive that holds workers to their tasks, and contradiction is the natural evolutionary spark of ideas.

Adventurers

As the category name implies, these *leaderless leaders* are consumed with adventure; they are out to push the envelope. Being productive is not exciting enough for adventurers. They are geared for the sensational. When cornered, they come out swinging with an incomprehensible explanation. Nothing is impeded by its possible consequences, as it never occurs to adventurers that they might get caught. They are often brilliant and could succeed without all the artful dodging, but it wouldn't be nearly as much fun. Often the adventurer is the darling of the organization, the daredevil and non-conformist that is envied for monstrous accomplishments that often seem unbelievable (and may be based on cutting corners, slipshod work, or outright fabrication).

Spin Doctors

Spin doctors see themselves as the eyes, ears, and voice of authority and their role to put the best possible face on the worst situation. These *leaderless leaders* tend to reduce everything to digestible sound bites, which often leads to credibility issues. Assessing explosive issues and putting a positive spin on them is no small achievement.

It requires the skill of the illusionist to change complexity into simplicity, give the chaotic situation an orderly context, and cloak crisis situations under the umbrella of calm. The danger is that spin doctors' short-term solutions often create long-term problems. Spin doctors are apt to be quick witted, congenial, decisive, and backstage performers.

Reluctant Soldiers

Everyone knows and tolerates reluctant soldiers without expecting anything from them. They are in the same job and at the same level where they started. They are *leaderless leaders* who wandered into a job and found a home. Long ago they retired on the job. They have received increased compensation and enhanced entitlements for doing less and less over the years. To call them lazy is an oversimplification. They are often crafty with an instinct for survival. When first employed, they were considered safe hires and then were forgotten. Statistically, they are part of the 15 percent foot draggers that plague most organizations.

Overachievers

Overachievers equate working hard without necessarily working smart. They pride themselves on their multitasking and fail to see its down side, and demonstrate surface acumen that garners the attention of superiors. It doesn't hurt that they are usually likeable, agreeable, and never seem to sleep. Their attractiveness blinds others from how little they achieve. No one seems to notice their obsessive attempt to cover all bases rather than to focus on the critical 10 percent causing the problem. These *leaderless leaders* are actually not achievers; they are well meaning but get lost in the detail. They equate accomplishment with time spent doing, and intensity of effort with competence. Overachievers personify a whirlwind process that far too often generates a marginal product.

Messiahs

Whereas unbending idealists dream of a utopian world where answers are not needed, *Messiahs* believe they have the answers. They provide corrective recipes to what ails the workforce, assuming motivation can be defined, packaged, and disseminated as a product — along with more appropriate styles of management — to rejuvenate a lethargic organization. The solutions presented by these *leaderless leaders* don't succeed because the culture dictates behavior, and the culture is driven by the structure and function of work and not by divine intervention. This requires architectural insight, which is missing in their answers.

Professionals

Professionals are a breed apart. They think in a language unique to their technology No entry level salary or job for them. They feel they have paid their dues in academia and now they are entitled. Somewhere lost in this scenario is the importance of experience, the benefit of failure in the learning process, and the realization that a career is a journey. *Professionals* want positions, not jobs; they desire authority without accountability. In an age when much work requires self-management, when maturity is essential to deal with ever changing and conflicting circumstances, these *leaderless leaders* epitomize the spoiled child that feeds on itself and the system. Campaigning for the next position is a full-time job.

Ten Guidelines for Successful Leadership

To move from *leaderless leadership to leadership,* workers and managers need to remember the following points:

- All contributions large and small are essential to an objective. All work is ennobling.
- No worker, manager, group, or function is complete within itself. Pulling together towards a common objective creates organizational synergy.
- Competitors are not the enemy. An obsession with killing the competitions saps the collective strength and derails effort from the objective. Much can be learned from competition because competitors are serving the

same customer.

- Technology should be user-friendly, available, and applicable as a tool to fit requirements, not as a toy to exaggerate differences.

- The best organization is not harmonious. Nor is the best employee the safe hire. A *Culture of Contribution* is the best design for success where struggle, failure, pain, disappointment, chaos, conflict, and confrontation are managed, as opposed to being avoided. What is a *Culture of Contribution?* It is organized chaos, a challenge to the existing status quo and modus operandi, and to misguided authority, and to the objectives that are inconsistent with the mission. It is also a challenge to do more than what is expected.'

- All organizations are in a state of dying. To survive they must constantly be reborn, retooled, and redirected. This requires a change in mindset and culture, which often results in a step backward before taking a step forward, a retrenchment to reassess the situation. In sports, we call it a time out, in life, we call it getting a second wind, in organization. We call it survival.

- Any organization is a human group. People are not things to manage but persons to be led. Leadership must encounter and deal with suspicion and questioning of authority in order to realize cooperation.

- People tend to compare and compete, to look at the "in" group and the "out" group, at the pecking order, on who is getting the perks and keeping score, and who is working and who is not. Given this tendency, there will be lapses — times when people won't be on the same page and times when the organization isn't working anymore. When this happens, don't bring in consultants or implement cosmetic changes; let the dust settle, re-evaluate where the organization is and how it got there. Don't point fingers, but apply strategic interventions that focus on the 20 percent causing 80 percent of the problems.

- The vertical structure of organizations isn't working. Nor is vertical thinking based on linear logic and critical thinking enough. Horizontal organizational structure is needed to complement the vertical structure. Likewise, lateral thinking, based on intuition and creative thinking, is needed to complement vertical thinking.

- Remember, organizational culture follows this formula:

Structure of work determines the function of work;

Function of work creates the workplace culture;

Workplace culture dictates organizational behavior;

Organizational behavior establishes whether an organization is to vegetate, flounder, expire or flourish.

Summary

Leaders don't know how to lead and workers don't know how to follow. The workforce has changed in the past 50 years from 90 percent blue collar to 90 percent white collar, but the mindset of management has changed little. Some feel the problem is management style, but it is not. Management, as it was paternalistically designed isn't working. Leadership is needed where workers are treated as partnering adults, not as dependent and obedient children.

Leadership is the vision to see and the ability to serve. To serve, leaders must become followers. They must understand the needs, desires, motivations, interests, fears, and dreams of workers —not by giving workers everything they request but by challenging them.

Every organization has the workers it needs to be successful. The problem is workers are reluctant to add their voices to the dialogue. Workers have the answers because they experience the problems!

These inclusive factors determine in large measure whether an organization has true leadership or *leaderless leadership*. They revolve around the three spheres of influence of the *Fisher Paradigm*™; workers and managers (personality), the organization (geographic), and the prevailing culture (demographic). Where does your organization fall in this continuum?

Resources

1. Ellen Goodman, "A Downsized Jack Welch," The Tampa Tribune, September 20, 2002, p. 17.
2. The News Hour with Jim Lehrer, "Executive Perks," Ray Suarez talks about pay and perks given to corporate CEOs with Rakesh Khurana, professor at the Harvard School of Business and Robin Ferracone, partner with Mercer Human Resources, PBS television, September 16, 2002.
3. James R. Fisher, Jr., *Six Silent Killers: Management's Greatest Challenge* (CRC Press 1998), pp. 7-21.
4. Fisher, op. cit. pp. 83-142.
5. James R. Fisher, Jr., *Work Without Managers: A View from the Trenches* (The Delta Group Florida 1991).
6. Edward de Bono, *Parallel Thinking* (Penguin Books 1995), pages 147-149.
7. Most organizations form a performance curve: 15 percent foot draggers, 70 percent followers, and 15 percent hard chargers.
8. Fisher, op. cit. pp. 197-220.

Note: This appeared in *The Journal for Quality & Participation,* Winter 2002, pp. 20-24.

CONCLUSION

A CONVERSATION WITH

STANLEY REEVES!

"In my youth I stressed freedom, and in my old age I stress order. I have made the great discovery that liberty is a product of order."
—**Will Durant,** prolific writer, philosopher and historian

"There is a history of leaders and groups who are ahead of their time, who resist prevailing trends, but who appear in the official documents as misinformed or mal-intentioned obstacles to the main direction of historical development. There is a history of common folk struggling to become, and becoming, their own leadership."
—**Frank Adams,** British mathematician

MANY PEOPLE have read this book in manuscript form, but none more closely than my dear friend, Stanley Reeves of Clinton, Iowa, a retired principal in the Clinton County School System. For

Stanley teaching was not work, but a labor of love. He dedicated his life in the service of others. He brought his heart and insight to everything he touched to the end of his days including this exchange with the author.

As school principal, he kept abreast of the changing maturations in education and, as you will see, not always without some skepticism. That is why I share with you his concerns expressed in a long letter to me after reading this book.

Stanley asks: One might assume that most workers want identity as well as financial reward for their work, but do most workers really want responsibility?

Workers as children shun the demands of responsibility. Such workers are non-responsible as opposed to irresponsible. They do what they are told and little more. Their greatest fear is to be exploited, so they exploit their employer, which is a punishing way of exploiting themselves. But mature adult workers, a breed apart and unhappily in short supply, are motivated by the challenges and demands of responsibility. It is the way they compute value and measure themselves.

Stanley sees contradiction in my suggestion that the HYPE (Harvard, Yale and Princeton Elitism) formula is not working. He agrees that Ivy League power brokers mainly represent the pomp and circumstance of the Establishment, the divine rights of insiders, and that HYPE has little motivation to modify the status quo, or to deal with society's sick soul. Therefore, he takes me to task for my failure to place our eroding society on HYPE, choosing instead to place it on the backs of workers, themselves. Why?

HYPE is far less important, far less crucial to society's redemption than HYPE, itself, would prefer to believe. HYPE is actually an aberration created by a passive society immersed in denial.

Obviously, HYPE has no real motivation to change conditions to a more optimum system, especially when it might prove threatening to its power. Why should it? As matters now stand,

HYPE reaps the benefits of passivity. A disenfranchised workforce and indifferent citizenry denies itself the power it actually possesses. Were workers to take charge of their destiny, the identity and recognition they so passionately desire would follow.

Modernity, or the processes of modern industrialism, has left workers running on empty. Materialistic society finds the glass half empty, not half full. Materialism's emphasis on consumption at the expense of spiritual nourishment has depersonalized relationships and crushed workers under the burden of a corpulent bureaucracy.

The predicted "death of God," or the "disenchantment of the world," however, has not taken shape. The hunger remains for balance between secular and spiritual needs. Only workers, themselves, can restore this balance.

Over his long career in education, Stanley has seen the repeated quest for the perfect formula in education. Each panacea has run its course only to be replaced by a new contender. It intrigues him that I should see "information technology" as essentially a new panacea, an excuse to avoid our problems. He writes,

"I found your concept especially interesting as all too often a professor writes a book and we all jump on his bandwagon. A few years later, we jump ship and adopt a new program. This 'new program' is not new at all, probably one that was dumped not that long ago."

I confessed to Stanley that I am not anti-science. Nor am I pro-technology for technology's sake. I am simply not awed by power brokers leveraging the newly discovered to fill their coffers.

My point here is that technology is not bad in itself, but that its promoters often use it as a ruse to gain control and influence, as well as economic advantage. Little thought is given to its long term impact on society. Science is the pursuit of knowledge, technology the pursuit of power. Technology, as wondrous as it is, cannot replace the spiritual needs of humanity. Man does not live by bread alone.

Stanley writes: "The segment on 'Silent Invasions' is so true, but sadly we seldom think about the fact that our lives are invaded from every direction...government, TT; surveillance, noise of every kind.

I love your expression, 'Love is the sinew missing from the muscle of today's organization... love of work, life, friendship, and being.

Lust, greed and pleasure are the void fillers for those afraid of love.' This is sad but true."

We are culturally conditioned from birth, programmed to value, believe and behave in a prescribed manner, a manner dictated by society. Conditioning is a powerful force with which few of us stop to wonder. It has enormous impact on our lives. Generations subjected to a particular style of cultural inculcation establish behavioral patterns, patterns which stubbornly refuse to desist when they are no longer appropriate.

Why are there no Catholic priests who are women? Why no American popes? Why has the United States never had a woman as president? *Alas, we have an African American president, who was not only elected in 2008, but also re-elected in 2012. And now in 2016, a woman, Hillary Clinton, is the Democratic Party's nominee for President of the United States.* Still, why so few great female philosophers? Why has work gotten a bad name?

Stanley's conditioning was revealed when he took exception to my claim that *"no matter where public confession is exhibited, it is suspect."* He sees the gross display of private lives on day-time television considerably more offensive than public confession in esteemed disclosure groups, such as Alcoholics Anonymous. I see them as both the same. They both rape the soul. He asks, *"Why do you feel that way?"*

When I was young, I thought electric shock therapy was barbaric; that frontal lobotomy surgery was uncivilized for the treating of the mentally ill. Yet, it was accepted as good, and I was told I was too young to understand otherwise. Earlier in our history, bloodletting was a prescribed medical procedure. It often hastened the departure of many souls from this life. To have suggested it was barbaric, then, would have met with a similar rebuke.

The sanctity of the human spirit is the last bastion of civilized existence. Too frequently, workers go along with violation of this sanctity for a "good," which they are told is greater than the evil it causes. So, they are silent. Their good sense is buried in a shallow grave, giving the benefit of the doubt to those deemed "wiser," but who are actually less attuned to the human spirit.

When we abuse our sanctity, it demeans the very nature of being human. There is nobility in private suffering, little grace in public confession.

In the chapter on "The Price of Innocence," Stanley asks: Are you saying that as empowerment comes from within rather than from things, we tend not only to accept giving up much control but to demand it?

What is intriguing about this question is that Stanley found the buzz word "empowerment" disturbing. It has thrown him off course. That is the intention of buzz words, to cloud the issue, cover-up the complexities, and let whatever inference is made be unchallenged. It keeps the dialogue going, nothing changes, and Madison Avenue has another marketing coup.

You are correct, empowerment does not come from "things." It comes from within. Power can only be given. Once given, it is nigh impossible to get it back. The current buzz word, "empowerment," is therefore totally misleading. Literature is replete with the issue of empowerment, as if this were a secret weapon from the *Oracle of Delphi*. Not so.

Management cannot "empower" workers. Only workers can empower themselves by grasping and using their own power. The only way one human being can have power over another human being is by one giving up power to the other.

"Empowerment" is one of those non-word words which periodically floats to the surface, like an oil slick, to pollute the cerebral cortex. No one can have power over another unless that person forfeits his power.

Democracy supports the myth that workers control their lives, when in fact they don't. People of influence flatter workers into giving up their power on a voluntary basis. This creates dependency and suspends workers in adolescence. Power, or control of workers' destiny is thus sacrificed for the promise of comfort, safety, security and harmony. Another word for "power" is freedom, and it is clear in these times of ubiquitous terrorists in the shadows of our lives that many are willing to sacrifice such freedom for the assurance of security and stability.

In totalitarian states, the same is done but on a more coercive scale. Far less consideration is given the mechanism of persuasion, which would have workers believe they control their destiny. Granted, there is a conspicuous difference in the ambience of these two political persuasions, while worker behavior is remarkably similar.

The similarity is demonstrated worldwide. In theory, if power is given up voluntarily, cooperation follows. If it is obtained through coercion, compliance follows. What behavior dominates the workplace worldwide? The evidence suggests that compliance prevails, which is cleverly masked to give the appearance of genuine cooperation.

Workers and managers everywhere proclaim they promote cooperation when, in fact, it is compliance. "Empowerment" remains a fictive machination which nobody buys, but everyone sells.

Technocrats feel they can bend and twist workers into the configurations desired that support the interests of technology. Empowerment is but one stratagem. Across the globe, sophisticated empowerment programs support technocratic objectives. They are not working. They cannot work. The stratagem is designed to fail because it plays recklessly with the worker's spirit, as if that spirit were a microchip. It isn't.

Workers gave up much of their power by the middle of the 20th century for the currency of comfort and security on the job. It created the working middle class. Up to and through *The Great Depression* of 1929, the "Robber Barons" of Rockefeller, Carnegie and Mellon, among others, took advantage of workers until they were little more than working slaves. Something had to give.

The Union Movement came to the fore, and fought hard for workers all through the 1930s, and gained compensation and entitlement concessions, but alas, at the expense of control of work. It had been a difficult transition from an agrarian society to an industrial society, and it is proving equally difficult going from an industrial society to an information society.

Farm workers were first chased into factories by the shift to an industrial society, and then regimented to time cards and imprisoned in windowless barricades called "factories." Not only did these farm workers surrender tractors and plows, but the freedom and control of what they did. As farmers, there was commitment to self-interests. Now, their lives were committed to a new breed, management.

Workers lost more than power. They misplaced their souls. Their identity, dignity and purpose, once taken for granted, was now stranger to them.

Seventy-five years of cumulative cultural shock has made workers passive participants to their own destiny. They are wards of "the system," no longer independent contractors. They can smell the fields as they drive to work, only to have the aroma killed by the stench of machine oil or the static hum of computers.

With a casual flair, management talks about "giving power back to workers" by "empowering them." This flippancy is like trying to put toothpaste back into the tube. Meanwhile, management itself has outlived its function and is disappearing from the workplace in droves. The Human Resources movement and its "scientific management" is obsolete. The worker is truly alone.

Stanley asks: How can we convince workers that in a number of areas we are no longer the best, when the government and media insist that we are?

This is not a problem of the government or media. Both are responsive, not creative organs of society. Workers give both of them far more credit than they deserve. The problem is the refusal of workers to embrace reality while they still have a choice. It appears they would rather deny despair, and surrender to a corrosive fatalism. Not until despair takes hold, and forces workers to attention will workers appreciate the fact that they are truly alone. Not until they hit bottom are they likely to challenge popular myths.

Maturity is a function of reality. Cognizance of reality ensures survival. When survival has multiple buffers, which make denial an alluring retreat, a sense of jeopardy is not experienced. Workers today live in a climate of denial, in the lap of luxury. They are only miserable, not yet despairing. They have little sense of danger, only inconvenience. The "other shoe" has not yet hit the pavement.

Stanley asks: Is it the amount of production or quality which deserves more of our attention?

It is heresy to suggest that these are not relevant considerations. Increased production means more jobs. Better quality means a more stable market share. Still, production and quality camouflage the issue.

These are outcomes or effects, not causes. What is ignored, and what I feel needs more consideration, is the necessity for workers to develop more orderly minds, like the minds they once had when they worked on the land from sun up to sun down, and loved it. Their minds were in balance with a sense of equilibrium. Workers today are underemployed because they are underwhelmed and underdeveloped. Tap this collective mind and the question of productivity and quality will be moot.

Workers are capable of incredible achievement if moved by their interests, or what they want to do. Focusing on production and/or quality exclusively are outcomes or things they have to do. Givens. Good quality and increased production are effects, not causes. The fusion of work is in the nuclear structure of the spirit of the workforce. Quality and production are the results of a spirited workforce built on trust with full utilization of its collective energies.

Stanley asks: Why isn't technology doing what we hoped it would do for education? Are our goals wrong our methods, or is it something else?

Technology cannot create spirit. It can kill spirit, and often does by the sheer magnitude of its conceit in minimizing the human factor. Spirit is the central core of work. Without it, work resembles a collection of mules turning a wheel and going nowhere.

Technology has limitation the same as everything else. In the end, the more technology seeks an answer to the mystery of the human spirit, the more it appears entangled in its own confusion.

Education is a spiritual adventure which is anchored in an intellectual experience. It is not a "thing," but a process. The process is one of discovery.

The human mind is seemingly limitless in its capacity for insight and foolishness. Tools, such as the computer, may assist in discovery as long as they remain tools and not as ends in themselves. Then they become toys, which is alright, too, as long as the distinction is clear. Where technology seems to be headed, at this moment, is as another ornament on the tree of knowledge. Nothing less. Nothing more.

What I see lacking in education is a philosophy of education. What appears instead is the expediency of design — a "new curriculum" for every contingency that surfaces. For me, the aim of education is to prepare the student first, to think, to become an able problem-solver within the context of life experience; second, the dual function to increase an awareness of the nobility of man's achievements, and an appreciation of the fragile beauty of nature; and finally, to make prudent choices in the student's best interest, which ultimately would prove beneficial to society.

This combination enhances the student's grasp of reality and maintains his hold on his spiritual legacy. The combination also heightens his capacity to love and to give of himself, which makes him more human.

Education is not preparation for a job. That should come later when the student chooses a profession, craft or vocation. All the technical skill in the world, without this spiritual-intellectual foundation, leaves little satisfaction. Life is meant to be lived, experienced, and enjoyed to fulfillment. Pain, risk, discomfort, embarrassment, confusion, doubt and failure are but country roads taken to arrive at that destiny.

Stanley asks: You speak of the control that polling has over our government as well as ourselves. What can be done?

In other books, I write that the "please other" mentality is damaging to the soul. Such a mentality is too easily swayed to follow the *Pied Piper of the Polls*.

When the focus is on other people's expectations for us (on their agenda), there is little appreciation of what gives us satisfaction. Life is a constant battle to please, in which case the spirit always loses: "You're damned if you do, and you're damned if you don't!"

Only by first "pleasing self" may the spirit soar and behavior be guided by what we personally think, believe, expect and value, not because we are instructed to be so inclined, but because we have discovered it to be so.

It is further suggested that this is one of our convenient masks that wins societal approval, but which hides a hidden agenda. It is the disguise of the victim, of the person who swims in the ocean of self-pity and never touches the shore.

On the other hand, the truly selfish person, who first understands and satisfies his basic needs, is more in a position to be generous and genuine. He is whole. Such a person values people who have an opinion, a stable of beliefs and a value system that supports those personal choices.

What a person thinks is of more value to him than what voices of wisdom would have him think. He bases his behavior on first-hand experience, not second or third hand information. He takes success and failure in stride. He judges others on the basis of what he experiences in his relationship with them. Celebrity, which the "please other" mentality spawns, is of no consequence to him.

Therefore, polls are irrelevant.

He has a point of view, a philosophy of life, an approach to the problem-solving. The choices he makes are his choices. He is a rare breed in our present corporate culture.

So much of identity and recognition is tied to collective belonging. Pollsters exploit this tendency. Many find comfort in thinking like the pollster's sample. One day it will dawn on those so inclined that the only person one can please is oneself. Advancing that agenda is bound to displease others. No one can have it both ways. Meanwhile, society is gridlocked in a nervous dance to be all things to all people. Polling is symptomatic of this mania.

Stanley asks: Where are students going to learn the difference between rights and privileges, since all too many parents have abdicated this responsibility? Many parents don't want schools to become involved in teaching values. So where does that leave us?

Forgive a personal aside. When my daughter was a teenager, we gave her the largest bedroom in our home, complete with her own television, personal telephone, stereo, bathroom, as well as generous access to a family automobile. I say "once," because she treated these privileges as rights.

Over time, as her behavior deteriorated, she was not grounded, but these privileges were reduced. First, she lost her large bedroom with adjoining bath. She had to find a place for most of her things in the attic as the new bedroom was quite small. In time her bedroom looked like a convent cell, with no phone, sparsely furnished, and she no longer had the use of an automobile.

After a few months, as her behavior improved, these privileges were gradually restored, eventually she was even given the title to her own automobile. She now understands the difference between "rights" and "privileges." School, which was once a drag, became important to her. She is now a college graduate and a successful professional in her chosen field. And she has done it all on her own. No one else can take credit for her turnaround.

You cannot teach values. You have to internalize values. Rhetoric is no substitute for the pain of reality. Neither parents nor teachers can have it both ways. Parents cannot threaten to take away privileges, then restore them without reason. Likewise, teachers cannot advocate values and then fail to demonstrate them in the conduct of their function.

Teachers often are afraid to be teachers. They complain they lack the support of the administration. Parents are afraid to be parents. They fear their children won't love them, will no longer see them as "friends." The result is chaos both on the home front and in the classroom.

Stanley writes: You ask who is to blame, then say, 'The workers have no one to blame but themselves.' Where does leadership come from? Is it any more apt to come from union leadership than the company CEO?

We are in the midst of a leaderless society. The role of leadership has not changed. Leadership remains a function of vision and service to others. That said transactional and transformational leadership, what scholars have focused on, is also proving inadequate in addressing the role of leaderships in the 21st century.

For some time now, those in positions of leadership, seemingly mystified by the new demands of leadership, have come to treat perks as divine rights, and to exercise power however they desire. Paradoxically, they have little sense of the nobility of their role. This is true in trade unions, academia, government, the religious, and the corporate world alike. They see their roles as *directors of activities* when it is primarily the *facilitation of consensus objectives in a climate of trust.*

Leadership has been on holiday, and gridlock has come to occupy the vacuum. The prerequisite for leadership according to scholar James MacGregor Burns is complete followership—that is, being attentive to the nuances and motivations of the human group. Today, leaders and followers, however, exist as if on different planets.

Patriarchal conceit springs from the belief that leadership is omniscient, that it knows what is best for workers without knowing them at all. This conceit has finally run its course. The fact that industry and commerce are stumbling along without leadership indicates how valueless leadership has become.

Psychoanalyst Karen Horney shows in her pioneer work, *Feminine Psychology* (1967), that it is time to cease and desist in seeing and coding everything in the problem solving from an exclusively male dominated perspective.

She advocates in her *leadership paradigm* that the female perspective is equally relevant especially in these revolutionary and transitory times. Alas, she suggests that men as well as women can utilize the *feminine paradigm* in the problem solving and, indeed, actually do so when they utilize both sides of their brains.

In other words, the complement of lateral thinking with vertical thinking or the intuitive with the cognitive is the perfect foil to gridlock. That is because such a compensatory adjustment is inclined to greater awareness and more maturity.

Society is surviving with no one at the helm but silent and dutifully employed men and women. Having said that, workers are still waiting for a venerated leader to rescue them from the *Limbo of Despair*. It will never happen. They expect from leadership what they refuse to expect from themselves. The result is stagnation.

Leaders do not choose their destiny. It is chosen for them, and by their followers. Leadership entails the heart, soul and mind of followers, the ability to mobilize their passions by uncovering their consensus needs, which are often beyond language. It is not the leader's agenda that is central to leadership, but its symbology. George Washington was not the great wit of his day, but he understood the people of the young American nation. He dressed like a leader, indeed, some said like a king without acting like one. He designed his own uniforms and they were gaudy and ostentatious. It was what the people wanted. His appearance connoted strength, power and purpose, symbolisms of leadership. Standing six feet two, straight back, firm jaw, and bold demeanor, he embodied what Americans took to personify their own character, their own strength and purpose.

For a good part of the 20th century, we have had it "ass backwards." Leadership develops its agenda and then recruits followers to mobilize support. This stratagem continues to fail for it is a counterfeit process.

Leadership rises out of the ashes of the Sphinx in the ritual of rebirth and resurrection. All of the trauma workers have experienced in the past several years could have been anticipated. Indicators of ensuing problems in personnel displacement and company retrenchment were glaringly predictable. Nobody paid attention, especially the workers.

Four people were assigned to do a one person job. Reports were generated which nobody read. Meetings were conducted on a daily basis in which 90 percent of those in attendance were subbing for those called to the meeting. Trips were taken as social jaunts with a wink at business. Hourly workers huddled in factory tunnels waiting for the whistle to blow for the shift to change so they could clock in for overtime.

When workers complained, they were careful to complain

amongst themselves, not to management. Meanwhile, workers didn't see themselves as part of the problem and therefore not part of the solution. Workers share in the blame and cannot expect relief from the problem until they accept this fact.

Without workers, there is no organization. Without dedicated workers, there is no good will or successful outcomes. An organization can survive with leaderless leadership at the top, as it has, but not without conscientious workers. Modern society is proof of this.

Stanley writes: You list three crucial flaws that contribute to the social psychological chaos of our times: workers failure to grow up and seize the moment; workers predominantly as knowers, not learners; and workers obsessed with control. You say happy workers are the foundation of a rational ordering society, then go on to say that this responsibility belongs to workers, alone. I quote, "Happiness is about being not becoming which is a choice."

My point is that the purpose of life is what we do, as individuals, not what we "are going to do," or "should do," or "are expected to do," or "say we'll do," but what we are actually doing, now.

Moreover, intelligence or brilliance is not a "genius" score on an I.Q. test, or a perfect S.A.T. score, intelligence is what it does. Potential is of little value if it is not translated into something meaningful and useful.

Once we are born we are old enough to die. Every moment of life is precious. Pain and pleasure, happiness and sorrow, success and failure are the fabric of meaningful existence. You cannot have one without the other. Every honest pursuit in life is noble.

None is nobler than another. If what we do is enjoyed for itself, gives us a sense of pleasure, is of value to others, and makes our spirit soar, we are on the right track to happiness.

Yes, it is a choice. Life is to be taken seriously, but not ourselves. There is a certain irony to everyone's life. The fool is as much a part of the sage as darkness is a part of light. Knowing this generates perspective, a sense of humor, balance, and secures our well-being.

Stanley had trouble with the chapter on "Not Happy Campers." *He writes: Weren't you painting society in general and special groups in particular with a wide brush? There are those in every trade and profession who take money under false pretenses. True, I have known teachers and professors who fit your characterization, but there are many others who are very dedicated.*

As to doctors, Dr. Bernie Siegel says that a large number of doctors need to remember to treat the patient as well as the disease. As to society two hundred years ago, sheer numbers make this a different world. A strong work ethic then was necessary for survival. Those who had a trade developed great pride in their work. As to how CEOs are selected, I suspect that in all too many cases what you assert is true. In government we seem to be so dumb that we vote for candidates who promise us the most without giving pause to consequences."

Only the reader can decide how wide my brush is. I share only my own experience, observations, reflections and limited knowledge. It is up to the reader to compare this with what he knows and understands to be so. If it fails to make sense, or fails to provide insight, then it will be rejected, as it should be. But if it touches a cord of experience and stimulates thought, it might increase the level of awareness and discernment. Then, reader and writer have connected.

Stanley writes: "It isn't likely a corporate board in New York City will have a personal interest in an individual in Clinton (Iowa) who works for the company. Doesn't the worker need to be part of the decision-making process at the operating level? Shouldn't he fight for that right as much as for more money and perks?"

Yes, yes, yes! But this takes education. It doesn't happen by osmosis. Money is the magic elixir of a materialistic society. It is the alchemist's gold. And gold is the standard by which everything is measured in a world of excess. After the basic needs of workers are met, however, money becomes the substitute for failed achievement, recognition, identity, purpose and influence.

Involving workers in the decision-making process is now critical to operations. There is no other alternative. Expediency demands such input. It also provides the recognition and identity that workers seek. Alas, poetic justice! So, why the problem?

Millions of words celebrate self-management work groups and workers as integral to the decision-making process, yet this connection fails to take hold. Why?

Workers and managers still do not trust each other. They see themselves as different, and so partisan hostility and self-interest continue to dominate the workplace. Logic never rules the heart, and the heart has a long memory. Time, patience and a supportive strategy are necessary to place the head and heart on the same body.

Stanley writes: Isn't it important for management to show up where the real work takes place? Don't they need evidence that they know what they are talking about? How many professors could step into a public school classroom and teach?

Yes, it is important. But that is not how the game has been played, until now. With adversity, there also comes good fortune. Management, as we know it, is anachronistic for reason.

Managers as a profession, for the past fifty years, have been essentially expediters and paper pushers. The nostalgia of their role in World War II never was relinquished.

Nostalgia for that mythic time simply grew like a cancer, metastasizing through every fissure of the organization's body until it was bloated with the dysfunctional malady of "corpocracy," and on every kind of support system, chief of which was the Federal Government's Department of Defense. I worked as an organizational development psychologist for a Department of Defense subcontractor.

For every ten workers, there was a supervisor, for every three supervisors, a manager, for every four managers, a director, for every five directors, a vice president, and so on. Workers were lost in the equation. All the perks and career ladders were set aside for this august group. Even engineers, who were critical to high tech success, remained outside the equation. When managers weren't pushing papers, they were in meetings or traveling to meetings. Meetings took up about seventy five percent of their time. While bloat was a corporate condition, purposeful meetings were suspect. This left little time for managers to manage "by walking around." When managers did, they invariably got in the way of productive work.

Necessity is changing this. *Non-doing of non-thing things* is a luxury the workplace can no longer afford, as position power has been usurped by knowledge power, and that is primarily possessed by workers. If managers don't have the appropriate skills today, or cannot relate meaningfully to workers, they cannot manage successfully.

Managers are part of a team, not apart from workers, but integral to them in the sharing of common objectives. Previously, nearly everyone in the chain of command eventually rose to the level of incompetence. This is a luxury that the organization can no longer afford.

How could it be otherwise? Managers only had so much time and that time was devoted to activity as an end in itself, not results. Moreover, they were prone to delegate what baffled them, and hold zealously to what they knew. This could only lead to chaos which it often did, reducing managers to pawns of departmental manipulators.

Manipulation is still the predominant norm in most organizations, in the public as well as private sector. There is a crack in this mirror. The tens of thousands of middle managers now walking the streets without jobs, the scores of former CEOs whose phones no longer ring, and the college presidents and professors, who are being shredded, have much in common.

They gravitated to the role of campaigners, always looking for the next opportunity with little time to deal with matters at hand, or the job they were paid to do. Now, they sit in the offices of headhunters writing resumes.

Stanley writes: Wouldn't management and workers get along better if they trusted each other? Apparently, the motive of each is suspect. It is probably true that the larger the business, the truer that is.

Yes, managers and workers would get along much better if they trusted each other. Trust must be earned. Once earned, it must be supported with consistency. If it is not, trust once broken is close to irredeemable. Trust is a fragile but powerful force in creating and maintaining organizational synergism. Nothing is impossible when there is a foundation of trust in the group. It can overcome adversity, failure, disappointment and even natural disaster.

Trust involves risk. Risk involves the possibility of pain. Someone has to take the first step, and mean it with his whole heart and soul, appreciating the vulnerability. Yet trust has little to do with organizational size. Once trust has been established, even a very large organization can literally erase competition.

Sam Walton did this by entering a saturated market with his Walmart store. He convinced workers and customers alike that he had their best interests at heart, then went on to prove it.

K-Mart, a company in a similar business, broke its trust. It secretly devised a 20/40/60 rule: review all twenty year employees for possible separation; review the status of all employees over forty for possible downgrading or separation; and review all employees making $60,000 or more for possible downgrading or separation. The plan was exposed. That was only a few years ago. Recently, this chain announced the closing of more than one hundred stores and the furloughing of several thousand workers and managers.

As striking as this example, distrust proves the rule rather than the exception (e.g., General Motor's ignition switch cover-up in 2014). This is because many organizations continue to have a cavalier attitude toward the trust issue. Alas, little learning seems to have taken place.

The chapter on "A Question of Control" generated this comment from Stanley:

"I wish we could think of the controller as the leader. It is my belief that the majority of people will respond to good leadership. They resent being managed. . . controlled. You suggest a changed society may take a century. Are we sure enough of the right course? Can we remain firm of resolve for that long? Not trying doesn't present a very pretty picture. It seems a given that to succeed managers and workers must share each step of the process. As to consultants, shouldn't they be part of the process instead of outside it?"

With control, as with everything else, it starts with the individual. The individual is the controller, or the leader of himself, if you prefer, or of that which he controls. The two cannot be separated. The individual cannot depend on a "leader" to rescue him from chaos and disorder. It is his individual responsibility. A leader can only symbolize what is already established. There are no miracles. Should this be construed as minimizing the traditionally understood power of the leader, per se, in leadership, so be it. Leadership has attempted to buy, bargain, cajole and/ or coerce workers into the desired behavior without success. The quest for freedom, control and order rests with working women. Why? Because they know the power of control without being the focus of such control.

Looking at control in the macro sense, I recall an advertisement for a brand of brown sauce popular in England several years ago. The advertisement showed Daddy bringing a bottle of sauce to the table. On the label of the bottle was a picture of Daddy bringing a bottle of sauce to the table, and within that label was a label that showed daddy bringing a bottle of sauce to the table.

Control is a sequential product of order, and order comes from within, one person at a time. The multiple of this process leads to communal order.

Everything is connected. The macro is precisely the same as the micro, only many times more. A true leader knows this in his bones. The structure of the human cell mirrors the universe. We explore the micro to understand the macro.

A "changed society" is an evolutionary process, which starts with an idea. There is no ideal plan or strategy to the growth of an idea. It is a factor of climate, opportunity and time. An idea may undergo several mutations before maturity is reached and bear little resemblance to the initial idea. There is no "right or true" course, only movement from moment to moment.

Ideas have a growth period the same as every other living thing. It is slow and tortuous with no clear path to the future. Ideas grow like cracks in the cement as weeds, wild flowers or grass. One day an idea experiences a transmutation from a puzzling perturbation into a clarifying insight that resonates with meaning to the times, which is not unlike a shoot bursting into bloom as a beautiful flower. Ideas are not separate but part of nature.

As for consultants, they are bystanders. Like multifaceted sensors, they derive their function from listening and observing. The answers are not with them, but are the filtered product of the organization's collective mind, a mind which is often ignored until a consultant repeats its intrinsic wisdom. Consultants provide connection between organizational knowers and learners.

Consultants are symptomatic of a culture that doesn't trust itself, a culture willing to pay for "a second opinion." Companies insist on seeing the controller and the controlled as separate entities. Consultant are often the arbitrary intermediary between the controller (management) and the controlled (workforce), which is a contrived dichotomy and therefore inauthentic. Were society not so uncertain of its priorities and ambivalent on how to handle them, consultants might just fade away.

Stanley writes with regard to the chapter, 'A Life Without A Cause": Can't change be a combination of outside forces as well as inside forces? Does it always have to be either... or? Wouldn't it be desirable for some things to come true that workers expect to come true, not because they expect it, but because they are desirable?

Change is always a combination of inside and outside forces. That is not the problem. The problem is what initiates the change process, stimulus from outside or motivation from inside? Chaos and order are part of the same whole. This dynamic created our universe.

Order starts with the individual deciding to change, to put his house in order, and therefore the change process is an internal commitment. Change is a reply to the demands of reality or outside forces.

What precipitates change is usually some disturbance, something that makes the individual or the company more alert. Attentiveness is the precursor to change. The decision to act is a response to that stimulus — take a death in the family. That was the case with me.

My father died three days past his fiftieth birthday. His whole life was one of repeated labor to push the stone of Sisyphus up the hill, only to have it roll back downhill and crush him again and again. He never had his own agenda. He was afraid to. He had great physical courage, but little moral backbone. It was impossible for him to take a stand if his rights clashed with the rights of his "betters."

With his death, my insides changed almost immediately. A cautious, conservative, sensitive person launched an immediate pilgrimage to gamble on himself, to do what his lights would have him do, and to let the chips fall where they may.

Thus was born my motivation to plant seeds that others were too timid to plant, or who feared it might lose them friends and jeopardize their careers. I am not constrained by such considerations. Nor am I concerned with whether these seeds reach fruition within my lifetime. I am a planter, not a harvester. My father's death convinced me of that fact.

Each worker has to decide who and what he is. If he doesn't, it will be decided for him. Desirable things come out of purposeful behavior. The purpose of life is to live it. How each of us might choose to live it is an expression of that purpose. The rest is academic.

FINAL WORD

"The Ascent of the Working Woman!"

THE ASCENT OF THE WORKING WOMAN is not new. Indeed, it is as old as time, as women have always been the gauge of the health of society, not men. Women have led without power using their guile to influence men when men were otherwise preoccupied to the point of walking off the cliff and into the abyss.

Women have been forced not to think of themselves but to be obliging listeners and partners to men, who traditionally have held the power, assuming a passive role to realize significant economic and social well-being.

When women have acquired power, they have been less inclined to "strut their stuff" in mocking imitation of male self-aggrandizement. Instead, they have been more disposed to husband their resources in the climb to financial equity giving rather than taking credit along the way.

That said the working woman is as capable of rational thinking as the working man, but makes no apology for complementing such thinking with insight from instinct and intuition, while knowing that she is married to the same machine as the working man.

Henry Adams (1838-1918) in *The Education of Henry Adams* (1905) anticipated this dilemma. This classic work, published posthumously in 1919, was acclaimed by *The Modern Library* as the top English language nonfiction book of the 20th Century. He writes:

The story was not new. For thousands of years women had rebelled. They had made a fortress of religion -- had buried themselves in the cloister, in self-sacrifice, in good works – or even in bad. One's studies in the twelfth century, like one's studies in the fourth, as in Homeric and archaic times, showed her always busy in the illusions of heaven or hell – ambition, intrigue, jealousy, magic – but the American woman had no illusions or ambitions or new resources, and nothing to rebel against, except her own maternity; yet the rebels increased by millions from year to year till they blocked the path of rebellion. Even her field of good works was narrower than in the twelfth century. Socialism, communism, collectivism, philosophical anarchism, which promised paradise on earth for every male, cut off the few avenues of escape which capitalism had opened to the woman, and she saw before here only the future reserved for machine-made, collective females.

From the male, she could look for no help; his instinct of power was blind. The Church had known more about women than science will ever know, and the historian who studied the sources of Christianity felt sometimes convinced that the Church had been made by the woman chiefly because it was feminine. After the overthrow of the Church, the woman had no refuse except such as the man created for himself. She was free; she had no illusions; she was sexless; she had discarded all that the male disliked; and although she secretly regretted the discard, she knew that she could not go backward. She must, like the man, marry machinery. Already the American man sometimes felt surprise at fining himself regarded as sexless; the American woman was oftener surprised at finding herself regarded as sexual (pp. 446-447).

One in reading this cannot but feel the prescience of these words. The *velvet glove* of the woman has yet to slide comfortably over the *iron fist of* the man while both have had no other option than to become married to the machine.

The skill base of the woman is proving more appropriate than that of the male as it is less fixed and more fluid, more adaptable to the new in radically different ways. But at the same time, it remains fully complementary to the skill base of the man. We go forward knowing it is essential that the man and the woman treat each other as equals, as persons with respect, and not as objects to exploit or demean. Survival is in the balance. That was a concern some one hundred years ago as historian Henry Adams so dramatically proposed, and it is likely to remain the concern henceforth for the next hundred years.

SELECTIVE BIBLIOGRAPHY

Jeffrey B. Abramson, *Liberation and Its Limits: The Moral and Political Thought of Freud,* The Free Press, New York, 1984.

Alfred Adler, *The Individual Psychology of Alfred Adler* (edited by Heinz L. Ansbacher and Rowena R. Ansbacher), Basic Books, New York, 1956.

Frederick Lewis Allen, *Only Yesterday: An Informal History of the 1920's,* Perennial, New York, 1964.

Walter Allen, *Tradition and Dream,* Hogarth Press, London, 1986.

Nancy C. Andreasen, *The Broken Brain: The Biological Revolution in Psychiatry,* Harper & Row, New York, 1984.

David 0. Arnold, *The Sociology of Subcultures,* The Glenessary Press, University of California, Santa Barbara, 1970.

Simon Baatz, *Knowledge, Culture, and Science in the Metropolis: The New York Academy of Sciences, 1817-1970,* New York Academy of Sciences, 1990.

Russell Baker, *Growing Up,* Signet, 1982.

J. Arthur Baird, *The Greed Syndrome: An Ethical Sickness in American Capitalism,* Hampshire Books, Akron (Ohio), 1989.

Donald L. Barlett and James B. Steele, America: *What Went Wrong?* Andrews and McMeel, Kansas City, 1992.

J. A. Barnes, *A Pack of Lies: Towards a Sociology of Lying,* Cambridge, Great Britain, 1994.

William Barrett: *Irrational Man: A Study in Existential Philosophy,* Anchor Books, 1962. *Death of the Soul: Philosophical Thought from Descartes to the Computer,* Oxford University Press, 1987. *The Illusion of Technique: A Search for Meaning in a Technological Civilization,* Anchor Books, 1979.

Jacques Barzun, *The House of Intellect,* Harper Torchbooks, New York, 1961.
Gregory Bateson, *Steps to an Ecology of Mind,* Ballantine Books, New York, 1972. *Mind and Nature: A Necessary Unity,* Fontana Paperbacks, Great Britain, 1985.
Ernest Becker, *The Structure of Evil: An Essay on the Unification of the Science of Man,* George Braziller, New York, 1968. *Revolution in Psychiatry: The New Understanding of Man,* The Free Press, New York, 1964. *The Birth and Death of Meaning: An Interdisciplinary on the Problem of Man,* The Free Press, New York, 1971. *Beyond Alienation: A Philosophy of Education for the Crisis of Democracy,* George Braziller, New York, 1967.
Willard and Marguerite Beecher, *Beyond Success and Failure: Ways to Self-Reliance and Maturity,* Pocket Books, New York, 1966.
Robert N. Bellah, et al, *Habits of the Heart: Individualism and Commitment in American Life,* University of California Press, Berkeley, 1985. *The Good Society,* Vintage Books, New York, 1992.
Ruth Benedict, *Patterns of Culture,* Mentor, New York, 1959.
Edward Bellamy, *Looking Backward,* New American Library, New York, 1960.
William J. Bennett, *The Index of Leading Cultural Indicators,* Touchstone Books, New York, 1994. *The De-Valuing of America,* Touchstone Books, N.Y., 1992.
Peter L. Berger, *The Sacred Canopy,* Anchor Books, New York, 1967. *The Homeless Mind: Modernization and Consciousness,* Random House, New York, 1973. *The Social Construction of Reality,* Anchor Books, New York, 1967.
Jesse Bering, *Belief Instinct: The Psychology of Souls, Destiny and The Meaning of Life,* W. W. Norton & Co., New York, 2012. Joseph H. Barked, *the Tyranny of Malice,* Summit Books, New
York, 1988.
Isaiah Berlin, *The Crooked Timber of Humanity,* Alfred A. Knopf, New York, 1991. *The Hedgehog and the Fox: An Essay on*

Tolstoy's View of History, Phoenix Paperback, Great Britain, 1992. *Conversations with Isaiah Berlin (& Ramin Jahanbegloo),* Charles Scribner's Sons, New York, 1991.

Bruno Bettelheim, *The Uses of Enchantment: The Meaning and Importance of Fairy Tales,* Vintage Books, New York, 1977. *Freud and Man's Soul,* Alfred A. Knopf, New York, 1983.

Robert R. Blake and Jane Srygley Mouton, *The Managerial Grid,* Gulf Publishing Company, Houston, TX, 1964.

Thomas R. Blakeslee, *The Right Brain,* PBJ Books, New York, 1980.

Allan Bloom, *The Closing of the American Mind: How Higher Education Has Failed Democracy and Impoverished the Souls of Today's Students,* Simon & Schuster, New York, 1987.

Robert Boguslaw, *The New Utopians: A Study of System Design and Social Change,* Prentice-Hall, Englewood Cliffs, N. J., 1965.

Daniel J. Boorstin, *The Decline of Radicalism: Reflection on America Today,* Vintage Books, New York, 1970.

Kenneth E. Boulding, *The Image: Knowledge in Life and Society,* University of Michigan Press, Ann Arbor, 1966. *The Meaning of the 20th Century,* Harper & Row, New York, 1964.

Lee Braude, *Work and Workers,* Praeger Publishers, New York, 1975.

Fernand Braudel, *The Structures of Everyday Life: Civilization & Capitalism 15th-18th Century,* Harper & Row, N.Y., 1979. D. W. Brogan, *The American Character,* Time, Inc., N. Y., 1956.

J. Bronowski, *The Identity of Man,* The Natural History Press, New York, 1971.

Harry Browne & Beth Sims, *Runaway America: U. S. Jobs and Factories on the Move,* Resource Center Press, Albuquerque, N. M., 1993.

John G. Burke and Marshall C. Eakin (eds.), *Technology and Change,* Boyd & Fraser, San Francisco, 1979.

Daniel Calhoun, *The Intelligence of a People,* Princeton University Press, 1973.

V. F. Calverton (ed.), *The Making of Society,* The Modern Library Series, New York, 1937.
Leonard Cammer, *Freedom from Compulsion,* Pocket Books, New York, 1977.
Jeremy Campbell, *Grammatical Man,* Penguin Books, Great Britain, 1982. *The Improbable Machine,* Simon & Schuster, New York, 1989.
Albert Camus, *The Stranger,* Vintage, New York, 1954.
Theodore Caplow, *The Sociology of Work,* McGraw-Hill, New York, 1954.
Fritjof Capra, *The Turning Point: Science Society and the Rising Culture,* Flamingo, Great Britain, 1987. *The Tao of Physics,* Flamingo, Great Britain, 1987.
Alexis Carrel, *Reflections on Life,* Hawthorn Books, New York, 1965.
Pat Choate, *The High-Flex Society,* Alfred A. Knopf, New York, 1986.
Harlan Cleveland, *The Knowledge Executive: Leadership in an Information Society,* E.P. Dutton, New York, 1985.
Harry Cohen, *Connections,* Iowa State University Press, Ames, Iowa, 1981.
Philip S. Cook, et al (eds.), *American Media,* Wilson Center Press, Washington, D.C., 1989.
David Cooper, *The Death of the Family,* A Vintage Book, New York, 1970.
Ralf Dahrendorf, *Class and Class Conflict in Industrial Society,* Stanford University Press, California, 1959.
Stanley Davis, *Future Perfect,* Addison-Wesley, New York, 1987. Terrence E. Deal & Allan A. Kennedy, *Corporate Cultures,* Addison-Wesley, Reading, MA, 1982.
John Dewey, *Human Nature & Conduct,* The Modern Library Series, New York, 1957.
Rosemary Dinnage, *One to One,* Penguin Books, N.Y., 1988.

Anthony Downs, *Inside Bureaucracy,* Little, Brown and Company, Boston, 1967.

Peter F. Drucker, *The New Realities,* Harper & Row, New York, 1989.

Emile Durkheim, *The Division of Labor in Society,* The Free Press, New York, 1964.

James M. Edie, *Phenomenology in America,* Quadrangle Paperback, Chicago, 1967.

Edward F. Edinger, *Ego and Archetype,* Penguin Books, Baltimore, 1973.

Howard J. Ehrlich, *The Social Psychology of Prejudice,* John Wiley & Sons, New York, 1973.

Albert Einstein, *bite-size einstein,* St. Martin Press, New York, 1996.

Ralph Waldo Emerson, *The Writings of Ralph Waldo Emerson,* The Modern Library, New York, 1950.

Desiderius Erasmus, *The Praise of Folly,* Hendricks House, New York, 1953.

Erik H. Erikson, *Young Man Luther,* W. W. Norton and Company, New York, 1962. *Childhood and Society,* W. W. Norton and Company, New York, 1963.

Charles Fair, *The Dying Self,* Anchor Books, New York, 1970.

Richard P. Feynman, *"What Do You Care What Other People Think?"* Bantam, New York, 1988. *"Surely You're Joking, Mr. Feynman!"* Bantam, N.Y., 1985.

James R. Fisher, Jr., *Work Without Managers: A View from the Trenches,* Tate Publishing Company, Mustang, OK, 2014; Corporate *Sin: Leaderless Leadership and Dissonant Workers;* Tate Publishing Company, 2013; *Time Out for Sanity! Blueprint for Dealing with an Anxious Age,* Tate Publishing Company, 2015; *Who Put You in the Cage? NOWHERE MAN IN NOWHERE LAND!* (Both 2016) Kindle Library, www.amazon.com; *Six Silent Killers: Management's Greatest Challenge,* Tate Publishing Company, 2014.

Robert Elliot Fitch, *Odyssey of the Self-Centered Self,* Harcourt, Brace &World, New York, 1961.

Robert Fishman, *Bourgeois Utopias: The Rise and Fall of Suburbia,* Basic Books, New York, 1987.

Arthur Fleischer, Jr., et al, *Board Games: The Changing Shape of Corporate Power,* Little, Brown and Company, Boston, 1988. Roy G. Francis, *Crumbling Walls,* Schenkman Publishing, Cambridge, MA, 1970.

Viktor E. Frankl, *Man's Search for Meaning,* Washington Square Press, New York, 1984.

J. T Fraser, *Time: The Familiar Stranger,* University of Massachusetts Press, Amherst, 1987.

Sigmund Freud, *Character and Culture,* Collier Books, New York, 1963. *The Future of Illusion,* W. W. Norton, New York, 1961. *Beyond the Pleasure Principle,* Bantam, New York, 1972. *Civilization and Its Discontents,* W. W. Norton, N. Y., 1961.

Herbert J. Freudenberger, *Burn Out: The High Cost of High Achievement,* Anchor Books, New York, 1980.

Thomas Friedman, *Up The Ladder: Coping with the Corporate Climb,* Warner Books, New York, 1986.

Erich Fromm, *You Shall Be As Gods,* Fawcett Premier Book, Greenwich, CT, 1966. *Beyond The Chains of Illusion,* Touchstone Books, 1962, *Escape From Freedom,* Rinehart and Company, New York, 1941. *Man for Himself,* Fawcett Premier, 1947. *The Forgotten Language,* Grove Press, New York, 1951. *The Revolution of Hope: Toward a Humanized Technology,* Perennial Library, New York, 1968.

Francis Fukuyama, *The End of History and the Last Man,* The Free Press, New York, 1992.

Robert C. Fuller, *Americans and the Unconscious,* Oxford University Press, New York, 1986.

John Kenneth Galbraith, *The New Industrial State,* New American Library, New York, 1967. *The Culture of Contentment,* Houghton Mifflin, New York, 1992 *The Affluent Society,* Mentor Book, New York, 1958.

Joshua Gamson, *Claims to Fame: Celebrity in Contemporary America,* University of California Press, Berkeley, 1994.

Barbara Garson, *The Electronic Sweatshop: How Computers are Transforming the Office of the Future into the Factory of the Past,* Simon and Schuster, New York, 1988.

Kenneth J. Gergen, *The Saturated Self: Dilemmas of Identity in Contemporary Life,* Basic Books, New York, 1991.

Eli Ginzberg and George Vojta, *Beyond Human Scale: The Large Corporation at Risk,* Basic Books, New York, 1985.

William Glasser, *The Identity Society,* Perennial Library, New York, 1976. *Reality Therapy,* Perennial Library, 1975. *Positive Addiction,* Harper and Row, 1976.

James Gleick, *Genius: The Life and Science of Richard Feynman,* Pantheon Books, New York, 1992.

Frank Goble, *The Third Force,* Pocket Books, New York, 1970.

Johann Wolfgang Von Goethe, *Goethe's Faust,* Anchor Publishing, New York, 1962.

Erving Goffman, *The Presentation of Self in Everyday life,* Anchor Books, New York, 1959. *Interaction Ritual,* Pantheon Books, New York, 1967.

William Golding, *Lord of the Flies,* Capricorn Books, New York, 1954.

Robert Goldston, *The Road Between the Wars: 1918-1941,* Fawcett Crest, New York, 1978.

Stephen Jay Gould, *The Mismeasure of Man,* Penguin Books, London, 1984.

Gerald Graff, *Beyond The Culture Wars,* W. W. Norton & Co., New York, 1992.

Robert K. Greenleaf, *Servant Leadership: A Journey into the Nature of Legitimate Power and Greatness,* Paulist Press, New York, 1977.

Richard B. Gregg, *The Self Beyond Yourself,* J. B. Lippincott Company, Philadelphia, 1956.

Martin L. Gross, *The Psychological Society,* Touchstone Books, New York, 1978.

Herbert G. Gutman, *Power & Culture: Essays on the American Working Class,* Pantheon Books, New York, 1987.
J. Eugene Haas and Thomas E. Drabek, *Complex Organizations,* MacMillan, New York, 1973.
David Halberstam, *The Reckoning,* Bloomsbury, Great Britain, 1987.
Jan Halper, *Quiet Desperation: The Truth About Successful Men,* Warner Books, New York, 1988.
Leslie A. Hart, *Human Brain and Human Learning,* Books for Educators, Village of Oak Creek, AZ, 1983.
Erich Harth, *Dawn of a Millennium: Beyond Evolution and Culture,* Little, Brown and Company, Boston, 1990.
Vaclav Havel, *Disturbing the Peace,* Alfred A. Knopf, New York, 1990.
Jules Henry, *Culture Against Man,* Vintage, N.Y., 1963. *On Sham, Vulnerability and Other Forms of Self-Destruction,* Vintage Books, New York, 1973.
Frederick Herzberg, *Work and the Nature of Man,* World Publishing Company, New York, 1966.
Craig R. Hickman and Michael A. Silva, *The Future 500,* Unwin Hyman, London, 1987.
Gilbert Highet, *The Art of Teaching,* Vintage, N. Y., 1950.
Stephen Hill, *Competition and Control at Work,* M.I.T. Press, Cambridge, MA, 1981.
Eric Hoffer, *The True Believer,* Time, Inc., 1963. *The Ordeal of Change,* Perennial, New York, 1963.
Karen Horney, *The Neurotic Personality of Our Time,* W. W. Norton, New York, 1964. *Neurosis and Human Growth: The Struggle Toward Set-Realization,* W. W. Norton, N.Y., 1950. *Are You Considering Psychoanalysis?* W. W. Norton & Co., New York, 1962. *Feminine Psychology,* W. W. Norton & Company, New York, 1967.
Robert Howard, *Brave New Work-Place: America's Corporate Utopias—How They Create New Inequalities and Social Conflicts in our Working Lives,* Viking, New York, 1985.

Aldous Huxley, *Brave New World,* A Perennial Classic, New York, 1946. *The Door of Perception/Heaven and Hell,* Harper Colophon Books, New York, 1963.

Ivan Illich, *Celebration of Awareness: A Call for Institutional Revolution,* Pantheon Books, New York, 1970. *Deschooling Society,* Harrow Books, New York, 1972.

Paul Johnson, *The Birth of the Modern: World Society 1815-1830,* Harper Collins, New York, 1991.

C. G. Jung, *The Undiscovered Self,* Mentor Books, N.Y., 1958. Franz Kafka, *The Trial* Penguin Modern Classics, New York, 1986.

Alan M. Kantrow, *The Constraints of Corporate Tradition: Doing the Correct Thing, Not Just What the Past Dictates,* Harper & Row, N.Y., 1984.

Glenn Kaplan, *The Big Time: How Success Really Works in 14 Top Business Careers,* Congdon & Weed, New York, 1982.

Paul Kennedy, *The Rise and Fall of the Great Powers: Economic Change and Military Conflict from 1500 to 2000,* Random House, N. Y., 1987.

Manfred F. R. Kets de Vries, *Prisoners of Leadership,* John Wiley & Sons, New York, 1989.

Tracy Kidder, *The Soul of a New Machine,* Avon Books, New York, 1990.

Orrin E. Klapp, *Collective Search for Identity,* Holt, Rinehart and Winston, New York, 1969.

Everett Knight, *The Objective Society,* George Braziller, New York, 1960.

Peter Koestenbaum, *Leadership,* Jossey-Bass, San Francisco, 1991. Arthur Kornhaber, *Spirit: Mind, Body, and The Will to Existence,* St. Martin's Press, New York, 1988.

Jonathan Kozol, *Illiterate America,* New American Library, New York, 1985.

J. Krishnamurti, *You Are The World,* Harper & Row, N. Y., 1972. *Commentaries on Living* (1st), Quest Book, Wheaton, IL, 1956. *Commentaries on Living* (2nd), Quest Book, Wheaton,

IL, 1958. *Life Ahead,* Quest Book, Wheaton, IL, 1963. *The First and Last Freedom,* Quest Book, Wheaton, IL, 1954. *The Awakening of Intelligence,* Avon Books, New York, 1973.

Thomas S. Kuhn, *The Structure of Scientific Revolutions,* University of Chicago Press, Chicago, 1962.

Douglas LaBier, *Modern Madness: The Emotional Fallout of Success,* Addison-Wesley, New York, 1986.

R. D. Laing, *The Voice of Experience,* Pantheon Books, New York, 1982. *The Politics of the Family,* Pantheon, New York, 1971. *Wisdom, Madness & Folly,* McGraw-Hill, New York, 1985.

Lewis H. Lapham, *Money and Class in America: Notes and Observations on the Civil Religion,* Ballantine, N. Y., 1988. *The Wish For Kings,* Grove Press, New York, 1993.

Christopher Lasch, *The True and Only Heaven: Progress and Its Critics,* W. W. Norton, New York, 1991. *The Minimal Self,* W. W. Norton, 1984. *The Culture of Narcissism,* W. W. Norton, 1978.

Harold D. Lasswell and Abraham Kaplan, *Power and Society,* Yale Paperback, 1950.

Kenneth Scott Latourette, *A History of Christianity,* Harper & Row, New York, 1953.

Lawrence LeShan, *The Dilemma of Psychology,* Dutton, N.Y., 1990.

Edgar A. Levenson, *The Fallacy of Understanding,* Basic Books, New York, 1972.

Harry Levinson, *The Great Jackass Fallacy,* Harvard, Boston, 1973. Sinclair Lewis, *Main Street,* Harcourt, Brace and Howe, New York, 1920.

Rensis Likert, *The Human Organization: Its Management and Values,* McGraw Hill, New York, 1967.

David C. Lindberg and Ronald L. Numbers, *When Science & Christianity Meet,* The University of Chicago Press, Chicago, 2003.

William L. Livingston, *Friends in High Places,* F.E.S., Ltd., New York, 1990. *Have Fun At Work,* F.E.S., Ltd., N.Y., 1988. *The New Plague,* F.E.S., Ltd., N.Y., 1986.

Mario Livio, *Brilliant Blunders,* Simon & Schuster, New York, 2013.

George C. Lodge, *The American Disease,* Alfred A. Knopf, N.Y., 1984.

Konrad Lorenz, *Behind the Mirror,* Harvest, N.Y., 1973.

David Lorimer, *Whole in One: The Near-Death Experience and the Ethic of Interconnectedness,* Arkana, New York, 1990.

Standford M. Lyman, *The Seven Deadly Sins: Society and Evil,* St. Martin's Press, New York, 1978.

Michael Maccoby, *Why Work: Leading the New Generation,* Simon and Schuster, New York, 1988. *The Games-man: The New Corporate Leaders,* Simon & Schuster, New York, 1976.

Brenda Maddox, *Rosalind Franklin: The Dark Lady of DNA,* HarperCollins, New York, 2002.

Bronislaw Malinowski, *Freedom and Civilization,* Indiana University Press, Bloomington, IN, 1960.

Herbert Marcuse, *One-Dimensional Man,* Ark Paperbacks, Great Britain, 1986.

Richard Marius, *Martin Luther. The Christian Between God and Death,* Belknap Press, Cambridge, MA, 1999.

Jay Martin, *Who Am I This Tune? Uncovering the Fictive Personality,* W. W. Norton, New York, 1988.

A. H. Maslow, *The Farther Reaches of Human Nature,* An Esalen Book, New York, 1971. *Religions, Values and Peak-Experiences,* Penguin Books, N.Y., 1976. *Toward a Psychology of Being,* D. Van Nostrand, N.Y. 1968.

William Masters and Virginia Johnson, *Human Sexual Response,* Bantam Books, New York, 1966.

Floyd W. Matson (ed.), *Being Becoming and Behavior,* George Braziller, New York, 1967.

Rollo May, *Power and Innocence,* W. W. Norton, N.Y., 1972. *Man's Search for Himself,* W. W. Norton, N.Y., 1953. *Love and Will,* W. W Norton, N.Y., 1969.

Tim McCarver and Alex Belth, *Stepping Up: The Story of All-Star Curt Flood and His Fight for Baseball Players' Rights,* Persea Books, New York, 2006.

Douglas McGregor, *The Human Side of Enterprise,* McGraw-Hill Book Company, New York, 1960.

Stanley Milgram, *Obedience to Authority,* Harper Torchbooks N.Y. 1983.

Neil Millard, *The New Industrial Relations?* Policy Studies Institute, Great Britain, 1994.

Adrienne Miller & Andrew Goldblatt, *The Hamlet Syndrome: Overthinkers Who Underachieve,* William Morrow, New York 1989.

Arnold Mindell, *Working on Yourself Alone,* Arkana, N.Y., 1990. Robert A.G. Monks, Nell Minow, *Power and Accountability,* Harper Business, New York, 1991.

Thomas Moore, *The Planets Within,* Lindisfarne Press, Great Barrington, MA, 1990. *Care of the Soul,* Harper Collins, N.Y., 1992.

Wilbert E. Moore, *The Conduct of the Corporation,* Vintage Books, New York, 1962.

Desmond Morris, *The Human Zoo,* McGraw-Hill, New York, 1969.

Jean Mouroux, *The Meaning of Man,* Image Books, N.Y., 1961. Clark E. Moustakas, *Loneliness and Love,* Prentice-Hall, Englewood Cliffs, N.J., 1972.

Robert Nisbet, *The Present Age: Progress and Anarchy in Modern America,* Harper & Row, New York, 1988.

Michael Novak, *The Experience of Nothingness,* Harper Torchbooks, New York, 1970. *Toward a Theology of the Corporation,* American Enterprise Institute, Washington, D. C., 1981. *The Spirit of Democratic Capitalism,* Simon & Schuster, New York, 1982.

Kenichi Ohmae, *The Borderless World: Power and Strategy in the Interlinked Economy,* Harper Business, New York, 1990.

George Orwell, *1984,* HarperCollins, New York, *2013.Homage to Catalonia,* HarperCollins, New York, 2012.

Cecil Osborne, *The Art of Understanding Yourself,* Zondervan Books, Grand Rapids, Michigan, 1971.

P. D. Ouspensky, *In Search of the Miraculous,* Harvest, N.Y., 1949. Albert Pepitone, *Attraction & Hostility,* Atherton Press, New York, 1964.

Charles Perrow, *Complex Organizations,* Scott, Foresman and Company, Glenview, Illinois, 1972.

Laurence J. Peter, *The Peter Pyramid,* William Morrow & Company, New York, 1986. *The Peter Principle,* William Morrow & Company, N.Y., 1969.

Thomas J. Peters and Robert H. Waterman, Jr., In *Search of Excellence: Lessons from America's Best-Run Companies,* Harper & Row, N.Y., 1982.

William Poundstone, *Prisoner's Dilemma,* Doubleday, N.Y., 1992. Richard Rabkin, *Inner and Outer Space, W.* W. Norton, N.Y., 1970.

Ayn Rand, *The Virtue of Selfishness,* Signet, N.Y., 1964.

Otto Rank, *The Trauma of Birth,* Harper Torchbooks, N.Y., 1973. *Psychology of the Soul,* Perpetua Book, N.Y., 1961.

Robert B. Reich, *The Work of Nations,* Alfred A. Knopf, New York, 1991.

Theodor Reik, *Listening with the Third Ear,* Pyramid Books, New York, 1965.

Jeremy Rifkin, *Entropy,* Bantam, New York, 1981. *Time Wars,* Touchstone Books, New York, 1989.

Carl R. Rogers, *On Becoming A Person,* Houghton Mifflin, Boston, 1961. A *Way of Being,* Houghton Mifflin, Boston, 1980.

Milton Rokeach, *Beliefs, Attitudes and Values,* Jossey-Bass, San Francisco, 1972.

Norman E. Rosenthal, *Seasons of the Mind,* Bantam, N.Y., 1990. Lillian B. Rubin, *Intimate Strangers: Men and Women Together,* Harper Colophon, New York, 1983.
Theodore Isaac Rubin, *Compassion & Self-Hate,* Ballantine Books, New York, 1975.
Jurgen Ruesch and Gregory Bateson, *Communication,* Norton Library, New York, 1968.
Hendrik M. Ruitenbeek, *Sexuality & Identity,* Delta Books, New York, 1971.
Bertrand Russell, *Education of Character,* Philosophical Library, New York, 1961.
Jean Paul Sartre, *Situations,* George Braziller, N.Y., 1965. Richard Schickel, *Intimate Strangers: The Culture of Celebrity,* Doubleday, New York, 1985.
Herbert I. Schiller, *The Mind Managers,* Beacon Press, Boston, 1973.
Arthur M. Schlesinger, Jr., *The Disuniting of America,* W. W. Norton and Company, New York, 1991.
Steven Schlossstein, *The End of the American Century,* Congdon Weed, New York, 1989.
Gary Schwartz, *Beyond Conformity or Rebellion,* University of Chicago Press, Chicago, 1987.
Albert Schweitzer, *The Philosophy of Civilization,* Macmillan Paperbacks, New York, 1960.
David Seabury, *How To Live With Yourself,* Science of Mind Los Angeles, 1984. *The Art of Selfishness,* Pocket Books, N.Y., 1974.
Roderick Seidenberg, *Post-Historic Man,* Viking, N.Y., 1974.
Steven Shapin, *A Social History of Truth: Civility and Science in 17th Century England,* University of Chicago Press, Chicago, 1994.
Jerome Shuchter, *Revolutionizing Reform,* Dorrance, Bryn Mawr, PA, 1987.
B. F. Skinner, *Beyond Freedom & Dignity,* Bantam/Vintage Book, New York, 1972.

Philip Slater, *The Pursuit of Loneliness: American Culture at the Breaking Point,* Beacon Press, Boston, 1970. *Earthwalk,* Anchor Books, New York, 1974.

Hedrick Smith, *The Power Game,* Random House, N.Y., 1988.

Page Smith, *Killing The Spirit,* Penguin Books, New York, 1990.

Robert W. Smith (ed.), *Guilt, Man & Society,* Anchor Books, N.Y., 1971.

P. A. Sorokin, *The Crisis of Our Age,* Dutton, N.Y., 1941.

Thomas Sowell, *Inside American Education,* The Free Press, New York, 1993.

Edward Stevens, *The Morals Game,* Paulist Press, N.Y., 1974.

Joseph Eugene Stiglitz, *The Price of Inequality: How Today's Divided Society Endangers Our Future,* W. W. Norton & Company, New York, 2012; *The Great Divide: Unequal Societies and What We Can Do About Them,* W. W. Norton & Company, 2015.

I. F. Stone, *The Trials of Socrates,* Little, Brown and Company, Boston, 1988.

Thomas S. Szasz, *The Myth of Mental Illness,* Perennial, N.Y., 1974. *The Manufacture of Madness,* Delta Books, N.Y., 1970.

Curt Tausky, *Work Organizations,* University of Massachusetts, Amherst, 1978.

Taylor, Frederick Winslow, "*The Principles of Scientific Management,*" W. W. Norton & Company, 1967.

Studs Terkel, *Working* Avon, New York, 1972.

William Irwin Thompson, *Imaginary Landscape: Making Worlds of Myth and Science,* St. Martin's Press, New York, 1989.

Alexis de Tocqueville, *Democracy In America* (Vol. I and II), Alfred A. Knopf, New York, 1945 [Reprint of 1835 edition].

Alvin Toffler, *Future Shock,* Bantam, N.Y., 1971. *The Third Wave,* William Morrow, New York, 1980. *Power Shift,* Bantam, New York, 1990.

Peter Trachtenberg, *The Casanova Complex,* Poseidon Press, New York, 1988.

Alan Valentine, *The Age of Conformity,* Henry Regnery, Chicago, 1954.
Clarence C. Walton, *The Moral Manager,* Harper Business, N.Y., 1988.
Sam Walton, *Sam Walton: Made in America (My Story),* Doubleday, New York, 1992.
Michael Walzer, *The Paradox of Liberation: Secular Revolutions and Religious Counterrevolutions,* Yale *University Press, New Haven, CT., 2015
James D. Watson, *The Double Helix*, New American Library, 1968, Haven, Conn., 2015.
Alan W. Watts, *Out of the Trap*, South Bend, IN, 1985. *The Wisdom of Insecurity,* Vintage, New York, 1951.
Max Weber, *The Protestant Ethic and the Spirit of Capitalism,* Routledge, New York, 2013.
Donald A. Wells, *God, Man and the Thinker,* Delta Books, New York, 1967.
William H. Whyte, Jr., *The Organization Man,* Doubleday Anchor Books, New York, 1956.
Keith D. Wilcock, *The Corporate Tribe,* Warner Books, N.Y., 1984. David Wise, *The Politics of Lying: Government Deception, Secrecy, and Power*, Random House, New York, 1973.
Robert Wright, *Three Scientists and Their Gods: Looking for Meaning in an Age of Information*, Times Books, N.Y., 1988.
Richard Saul Wurman, *Information Anxiety,* Doubleday, N.Y., 989.
Sam Walton, *Sam Walton: Made in America (My Story),* Doubleday, New York, 1992.
Michael Walzer, *The Paradox of Liberation: Secular Revolutions and Religious Counterrevolutions,* Yale University Press, New Haven, Conn., 2015.
Alan W. Watts, *Out of the Trap*, South Bend, IN, 1985. *The Wisdom of Insecurity,* Vintage, New York, 1951.
Max Weber, *The Protestant Ethic and the Spirit of Capitalism,* Routledge, New York, 2013.
Donald A. Wells, *God, Man and the Thinker,* Delta Books, New York, 1967.
William H. Whyte, Jr., *The Organization Man,* Doubleday

Anchor Books, New York, 1956.

Keith D. Wilcock, *The Corporate Tribe,* Warner Books, N.Y., 1984.

David Wise, *The Politics of Lying: Government Deception, Secrecy, and Power*, Random House, New York, 1973.

Robert Wright, *Three Scientists and Their Gods: Looking for Meaning in an Age of Information*, Times Books, N.Y., 1988.

Richard Saul Wurman, *Information Anxiety,* Doubleday, N.Y., 1989.

Yevgeny Zamyatin, *We*, Penguin Books, N.Y., 1993.

Bernie Zilbergeld, *The Shrinking of America: Myths of Psychological Change,* Little, Brown and Company, Boston, 1983.

Shoshana Zuboff, *In The Age of the Smart Machine: The Future of Work and Power,* Basic Books, New York, 1988.

Dr. James R. Fisher, Jr. in his study at home.

ABOUT THE AUTHOR

Dr. Fisher is an industrial/organizational psychologist who has worked across the United States, Europe, South America and South Africa with people at all levels of organization. He has been a corporate executive with Honeywell Europe SA and Nalco Chemical Company, while also consulting Fortune 500 companies and acting as an adjunct professor for several colleges and universities. He has written a score of books in the organizational development (OD) genre of which this is one. Check his e-mail at www.thedeltagrpfl@cs.com or his website at www.fisherofideas.com.

www.ingramcontent.com/pod-product-compliance
Lightning Source LLC
Chambersburg PA
CBHW020644220526

45464CB00001B/281